STYLE IN SILK HATS FOR SPRING.

AUTHOR & DRAMATIST

COPIED BY PERMISSION OF A. BASSANO ESQ 25, OLD BOND ST W.
(COPYRIGHT)

Offices. 19. Ludgate Hill.
London, E.C.

HAT MANUFACTURED BY MESSRS ROWLEY AND BROCK. LONDON. E.C.

If you have tears,

PREPARE TO SHED THEM NOW

Also by Arthur Calder-Marshall

WISH YOU WERE HERE

(the art of Donald McGill)

Prepare
To Shed Them Now
The Ballads of George R. Sims

**Selected
and Introduced
by
Arthur Calder-Marshall**

Hutchinson of London

Hutchinson & Co (Publishers) Ltd,
178–202 Great Portland Street, London, W.1.
London Melbourne Sydney Auckland
Bombay Toronto Johannesburg New York
First published 1968   Introduction © Arthur Calder-Marshall 1968
This selection of ballads by George R. Sims © Minty Lamb 1968
Designed by the Hutchinson Book Design Unit
This book has been set in Apollo by Oliver Burridge Filmsetting Ltd
and printed by offset litho in Great Britain
at Taylor Garnett Evans & Co Ltd, Watford, Herts,
and bound by William Brendon & Son, Ltd, Tiptree, Essex
09 0892003

LIST OF CONTENTS

ACKNOWLEDGMENTS

My thanks are due to many people who have helped me with this book; most notably Miss Minty Lamb and her agents Messrs Curtis Brown Ltd for permission to quote copyright material by George R. Sims; to Miss Lamb once again for allowing me to peruse her Simsiana and for giving me her recollections of her uncle; to her aunt Miss Wykes for corroborative and supplementary information; to Mr Ian Parsons for showing me correspondence between Sims and Chatto & Windus; to Mr Frank Swinnerton and Mr Oliver Warner for Simsian anecdotes; to the staff of The British Museum Reading Room and the London Library for assistance in research; to the Public Record Office and the Registrar of Companies for help in the elucidation of the Tatcho mystery; to The Guild Hall Bookshop Kingston and the Baldur Bookshop Richmond for help in finding some of the magic lantern slides used in the text and to Mr Edwin Smith for providing other slides, including that of the Babylonian Wonders in Ostler Joe (despite the fact that he was reproducing the full series in *The Saturday Book,* 1968); to Mr David Francis of Television Centre, for general information and in particular the quotation from *Readings in Prose and Verse* and finally to Miss Helen Macgregor, whose collection of ephemera (all bought for sixpence or under) gave me, among other gems, the advertisement for the George R. Sims Hair Restorer.

For permission to quote from *The Return of George R. Sims* I am indebted to my publishers, Messrs Hutchinson.

To Frances Maud Beatrice Wykes
alias
Minty Lamb, in gratitude

GEORGE R. SIMS

The Public Relation

Interviewed for *The Idler* in 1897, Sims remarked that he didn't want to go down to posterity. 'I want to go down well with people who buy papers, see plays, and read books at the present day. Mercenary? And who is it works for art's sake?' He was fifty and the Jubilee dinner given in his honour featured as a Savoury 'Billy's Roes on Toast,' in remembrance of the Ballad Billy's Rose, whose first line 'Billy's dead, and gone to glory—so is Billy's sister Nell:' had for nearly twenty years beguiled the simple by its poignancy and the sophisticated by its simpleness.

He was then at the height of his fame, a national figure; 'the nearest approach to Charles Dickens that we have had during the present generation. Indeed, he may be said to be the Elisha of that great modern prophet upon whose shoulders Dickens' mantle has fallen. His literary style; his enthusiasm for humanity; his intense hatred of oppression; his utter abhorrence of cant; his merciless castigation of the Stiggenses of the age—all these remind us of the great creator of *Nicholas Nickleby,* and yet *plus* the striking points of resemblance Mr Sims has an individuality all his own.'

Indeed he had.

He was the first, and perhaps the greatest, mass notability, the forerunner of columnists such as Agate and Beverley Nichols, or television personalities such as Malcolm Muggeridge or Patrick Campbell. At the age of thirty, in 1877, he had begun contributing to the newly founded Sunday *Referee* a causerie called 'Mustard and Cress' under the pseudonym Dagonet. This was something entirely new in English journalism. It was intentionally disjointed. It leapt from the grave to the gay, for public denunciation to private revelation, with the welcome relief of rows of asterisks.

But though it was an innovation in England, it was not the creation of George Robert Sims. He was not an originator in any field; merely a facile adaptor. Through Tom Hood Junior, the editor of *Fun*, a rival to *Punch*, he had met the satiric American journalist Ambrose Bierce.

In the San Francisco *News-Letter* Bierce had written the 'Town Crier' column, a new form of personal journalism, easy to read and hard to forget. He had continued it with 'The Passing Show' in the London *Figaro* and in *The Lantern*, a satiric irregular edited to further the politics of the exiled Empress Eugénie. 'Mustard and Cress' was Sim's version, tailored to suit the British public and his own blander, reformist personality.

George R. Sims wrote his 'Mustard and Cress' article every week for forty-five years. His last article appeared the Sunday before he died in September 1922; and even when Christmas fell on a Sunday and there was no issue of the *Referee*, he wrote the article all the same, for his own delight. It was a sort of public diary to which he confided his personal likes and dislikes, his public enthusiasms, indignations and curiosities and anything that tickled his fancy.

In consequence, his private life became more public than anyone's in England. For forty years, he lived in 12 Clarence Terrace, Regents Park, 'opposite the Ducks'. Such was the fame of Dagonet that a pictorial envelope addressed Mr with a drawing of a dagger and a lawn tennis net, London, reached him; as did one with a cartoon of his bearded face 'Opposite the Ducks'. This notoriety (from which the favourites of television to-day shelter behind dark glasses) Sims profitably cultivated. The poor man's Prince of Wales, he appeared on April 1, 1885 in *The Hatters' Gazette*, modelling Styles in Silk Hats for Spring, and in 1887 advanced to a full-length fur-lined overcoat in *The London Tailor & Record of Fashion*. The carriage builders Messrs Whitlock & Co built for him *The Dagonet Car* in which he trotted his ponies Sir Hugo and Faust Up to Date, with his four Dalmatians running beside. Since *Faust-Up-to-Date* was the title of one of his plays, the pony was a trotting advertisement. 'Alas!' he wrote in October, 1907, 'at a few minutes past eleven this Saturday morning Faust Up to Date . . . passed away after a few hours' suffering to the happy grazing lands . . . as good and gallant a little fellow as ever put hoof on a bit of English road, and for over 20 years my good friend and faithful servant.' All these were familiar to 'Refereaders', as Dagonet called them; as were the two bulldogs, Billy Greet and the prize-winning Barney Barnato, so named by permission of the millionaire, on condition that the dog did not disgrace him. The dog won prizes at every show where he was exhibited, until the millionaire disgraced *him* by committing suicide.

Licensed Victuallers' Gazette

AND
HOTEL COURIER.

| Vol. XLII. 1,300 | [REGISTERED FOR | FRIDAY, MAY 28, 1897. | TRANSMISSION ABROAD.] | PUBLISHED WEEKLY PRICE TWOPENCE. |

FAC-SIMILE

12, Clarence Terrace
Regent's Park
N.W

May 1ˢᵗ 1897

Messrs Spratts Ltd.

We the undersigned dogs
in common Council assembled at
opposite the Suckle Villa desire to
express our high approval of 'Spratts.'
We have lived on them all our lives
and when we ask for them we
see that we get them.

Signed. Lady Godiva
Slendon, Samson
Billy Greed, Barney Barnato
Pillar Palmer, Alfred Sewell
Primus, Fizzie

Their ✗ mark.

Witness to signatures
of above.

Geo Rhines

On May 28, 1897, George R. Sims and his dogs appeared on the front page of the *Licensed Victuallers Gazette,* Sims witnessing their canine testimony to the superiority of Spratt's Patent Meat Fibrine Vegetable Dog Cakes. The financial rewards for this may have been small compared with the modern T.V. Commercial, but the publicity contributed to that image of Sims as a figure of national importance, which reached its unfortunate apogee with Tatcho.

Tatcho was the product of The Geo. R. Sims Hair Restorer Co, Ltd floated on February 16, 1897. The nominal capital was £10,000, consisting of 200 £50 shares. The shareholders consisted of five journalists, two barristers at law, one publisher and two others whose combined knowledge of business might have had something to do with the production of a hair restorer, Charles Napier White, oil refiner and Henry Sarsons, vinegar brewer. Of the seventy-six shares issued, only one was held by Sims, who also contributed not merely his name, his hairy head and his assurance that with the aid of medical specialists he had discovered a cure for baldness but also the brand name Tatcho, an anagram of his publisher Chatto, of Chatto & Windus. But he was to receive twenty per cent of the nett profits.

There were high hopes of cleaning up a fortune, but, perhaps because none of these ten public benefactors was whole-heartedly or whole-headedly dedicated to the cure of baldness, The Geo. R. Sims Hair Restorer Co. Ltd. went into voluntary liquidation just over three years later on March 28, 1900.

The stock, the name and goodwill was taken over by a private firm of manufacturing Perfumiers, Low Son & Co, of 5 Great Queen Street, Kingsway, who also made Seeger'ol and Seeger's Hair Dye. They owned Sims's face, his signature and his Hair Restorer Company and they used it to the full. The original company had devised an 'Agreement to supply a hundred thousand Ladies and Gentlemen with a 4/6 bottle of Tatcho for 1/10.'

The new company could not put out fresh advertising copy using the face and signature of George R. Sims. So they continued the original advertisement, merely increasing the number beyond One Hundred Thousand. In the illustration on the end paper the number is 7692206.

If Sims had continued to receive twenty per cent of the net profits, his dignity might not have been outraged. As it was, he tried for years to have his name, whiskers and signature obliterated from the offensive advertisement. But he had no legal redress. He issued public repudiations, stating that he had no connection with the firm. But he could not deny that at one time he had tried to persuade the general public that he had discovered a cure for baldness or that the specific marketed as Tatcho was any different from the one he had originally sponsored. He was hoist with his own Hair Restorer; and as the twentieth century advanced and interest in his plays and ballads receded, he experienced the indignity of being famous not as the Dickens of his day but as the discoverer of Tatcho.

The popularity of 'Mustard and Cress', however, never diminished. It sold the *Referee*, and every Monday Sims would hold a post-mortem with the editor on how far the rest of the paper had fallen short of Dagonet.

Publicity works two ways. When Dagonet investigated palmistry, he had his hand read. So when other journalists followed suit, George R. Sims's palm was among those of the contemporary great. When Dagonet boosted Bexhill, Bexhill boosted Dagonet.

In the last year of his life, Sims's interest was enlisted in Spiritualism and Voice Mediumship. On December 12, 1921, Mr Saunders of Surbiton (a flyweight who had leapt to 9st 4lbs when he abandoned boxing in 1882) met Sims at Tufnell Park Station, both wearing buttonholes. As they walked to Colonel C's house for a seance, Saunders explained that his neighbour Mr M had been told by the ancient Persian, Abduhl Latif, 'You have the Pearl Ray, you must use it to help the sick.' 'The ray' Mr Saunders explained to Sims, 'is purely a physical adjunct and is an emanation from the body, rare, but not unknown in human beings, and, when used by the spirits, acts in a disinfectant and burning manner on the bad tissues of the body, and permits Nature herself to get to work and effect a cure.'

The first sitting at Tufnell Park was not very successful, partly because a third of the time was taken up by the effort of the spirits to satisfy Mr 'A' (the incognito given to Sims) and partly because 'Abduhl was at Surbiton Cottage Hospital'. But Dagonet gave it a mention in the next week's 'Mustard and Cress'.

In the first séance a Lancashire spirit called Joe Griffith sang, 'Oh, let us be cheerful' and joined in with the living at the end of 'That old-fashioned mother of mine'. At the second, the spiritual company was more distinguished. The shade of W. T. Stead remarked to Mr Saunders 'Our friend Sims here is a capital fellow. His eyes are not yet opened, but it will come.' He was followed by Mr Gladstone, who after a political harangue in which he said among other things, 'When we look down upon the masses constituting this great Empire, and know that God gave you victory, where, we ask, are the gratitude and the thankfulness for that great blessing? Where is the reign of the Brotherhood of Man which was to be inaugurated? Bolshevism is rampant . . . ' ended by confessing 'I was always interested in occultism, and I learned much from Queen Victoria.'

These amazing contacts with the spirit world were duly, if non-committally, reported in the *Referee*. But no further sittings were arranged because on July 5, 1922, Sims wrote Mr Saunders 'I am glad to say that I am slowly but surely getting on with the numerous diseases which have attacked me all at once.' On September 4 of that year he 'passed to the Spheres.'

But if Mr Saunders is to be believed, Sims the busy publicist turned up at a séance 18 days later. 'My dear old friend Stead and a host of others met me on my transition with smiles that went to my heart', he said. 'They took me by the hand and greeted me on my entry into the Spheres.'

Since Sims could not print his experiences 'after Crossing the Bar' in 'Mustard and Cress', Mr Saunders and 'a friend' published them for him in *The Return of George R. Sims* (Hutchinson), the rare and curious volume from which these quotations are drawn. He described his transition, his house, and his visits to his Poms 'Belle Brocade' and 'Peggy of the Potato Patch' in the Pets' Heaven. 'The colour of the dogs is exactly similar to what it is on your side, but their coats are more silky, more ethereal.' Before visiting the Christ Sphere with his spirit guide Emanuel, George R. Sims gave the inside story of the deaths of Mallory and Irvine on Mount Everest and launched a plea for the abolition of Capital Punishment. He had met the spirits of Adolf Beck and William Augustus Wyatt, the culprit of the thefts from prostitutes for which Beck was wrongfully jailed. 'Beck has gained some little extra position on this side for what he suffered wrongfully for on yours.' Mr Sims went on to say that he had visited 'the criminal classes' in the spirit world from the old days of Charles Peace to the present time. 'And how different it all is,' he remarked, 'how different are all the days that were from all the days that are.'' '

Always a sociable soul, Sims introduced departed celebrities to Mr Saunders and his friends.

'Good afternoon,' said a voice, emphasizing in a meticulous manner each syllable. 'My name,' he went on, speaking with more freedom,' is Augustus Harris.'

'What! Sir Augustus Harris?' a lady sitting with us asked.

'Well, we are not known by titles here,' he said.

Harris said he was trying to influence the policy of the National Theatre (at Drury Lane). 'We deplore the rubbish that is now presented at some of your theatres.'

Mr Saunders asked whether, when *The Return of George R. Sims* was published it would not be a good time to revive one of Sims's old plays, *Harbour Lights,* for example, or to inspire a new one on similar lines.

'There is no question whatever about it,' Augustus Harris replied. 'We are just as capable of writing a play at the present time as we ever were.'

But despite the otherworldly efforts of these celebrated shades, no new play, alas, was written by George R. Sims nor old ones revived in London, after he left the house Opposite the Ducks for the Summer Land of the Spheres.

Boy and Man

George Robert Sims was born in London on September 2, 1847 and died in London seventy-five years and two days later on September 4, 1922. In the interim he had sallies abroad, but he was always based on London, which he loved and wrote about prodigiously.

He had a strong sense of continuity, which is summed in a story of his babyhood. His maternal grandfather, John Dinmore Stevenson, was a leader of the Chartist movement; while his father, even as a young man, was a staunch upholder of the Establishment. So when in 1848, the maternal grandfather went to Kennington Common to lead a demonstration of Chartists to march on Whitehall, the father, enrolled as a special constable, went there also, armed with a truncheon, to prevent such an invasion.

The affair was disastrous. The heavens opened and drenched the forces of Law and of Disorder to the skin. So instead of using his truncheon, the father took John Dinmore Stevenson home to change his clothes, have a nice hot tea and admire the infant George Robert Sims.

The Radical and the traditionalist who stood together over his cradle became united over the baby; and the principles for which

7

G. R. S. at 21

G. R. S. at his Jubilee

'Dagonet's' House, Opposite the Ducks

Mrs. G. R. S. in dogcart

Sir Hugo at Home

they stood became harmonised in George Robert as he grew up.

As both his parents were young, John Dinmore Stevenson had far more charge of the early years of George Robert than is usual. George R. Sims was a lifelong Radical. And from his mother he learnt that it was possible for a woman to combine housewifery with social causes. She campaigned to raise the legal and social status of women and ended up as President of the Women's Provident League.

His father, a wholesale and export cabinet manufacturer and plate-glass factor, was a solid citizen. He had the freehold of historic offices in Aldersgate at London House, which had in earlier times been variously the town house of the Marquis of Dorchester, a State Prison during the Commonwealth and after the Restoration the palace of the Bishops of London. He gave his son a respectability which prevented his Bohemianism and Radicalism from ever being alarming.

It was a splendid inheritance. Though the Chartist grandfather belonged to the non-conformist sect of Sandemanians, Mr and Mrs Sims were anglicans, who combined wealth with good works, piety with a zest for living, and, most important of all, loved one another and George, the eldest of their six children.

George wasn't relegated to the nursery, while his parents enjoyed themselves. On November 18, 1852, he was taken to see the funeral of the Duke of Wellington. He had to get up at 4 am and by the time that historic occasion was over, the five-year old was so fretfully tired that to beguile him his mother bought a penny *Puss in Boots*. It shows his pride in continuity that he recorded that sixty-three years later he collaborated in turning it into a Drury Lane Pantomime.

At the age of six, his theatrical education began with a visit to Sadler's Wells to see Samuel Phelps in *A Midsummer Night's Dream*.

Even when he went with his grandfather to the Sandemanian Chapel in Hare Court, Barbican, he was making contacts for the future. What other journalist could boast of having heard the great Michael Faraday apologizing to the Sandemanians for having made a statement in a lecture to the Royal Institution which ran contrary to the teachings of the sect? The future song-writer met at the chapel the uncle of John Boosey the music publisher, and the future journalist of *How the Poor Live* drank Scotch broth in the chapel pews with the artist Fred Barnard, who was to illustrate those articles.

Everybody, of course, has chance meetings of this sort. But to George R. Sims they appeared, at least when he wrote *My Life* in 1917, to prove the singleminded progress of his development.

If one tries to imagine his career as he created it, perhaps it showed rather an alertness to seize every chance of fulfilling his ambitions, to live well in every sense and to write what people would like.

He went to schools in Islington, Eastbourne and Hanwell Military College. At this last, he edited the College Magazine writing in a rather subversive way, but for the last time in his life in a clearly legible hand.

In 1864, aged seventeen, he went to Bonn University. He spent an uproarious year, reading Balzac, translating Schiller into English verse, drinking too much and gambling more than he could afford. When he was arrested for an incident in a *lokale*, his father summoned him back to work in the Aldersgate office.

Young Sims loved the atmosphere of an office 'so Dickensian'. He enjoyed wandering through the City, but he couldn't take the work very seriously, because he was determined to be a writer. I think he was frank with his parents and his father decided that the sooner George could make a go of writing, the better it would be for his own business as cabinet manufacturer and plate glass factor. George began to lead the life of a young man about town, spending his nights in the pubs, clubs and houses in and around the Haymarket.

> The Haymarket was as busy as a fair all the long night through, and there were nighthouses in Panton Street and Jermyn Street and the streets around Leicester Square where you could drink bad spirits and worse wine till the early morning sun streaming in through the back-windows sent you shamefacedly home.*

George obviously had a wonderful time, arriving home with the milk, but rising with great effort of will to reach the office punctually in the morning. He lived in the family house in Hamilton Terrace, Maida Vale; and his parents must have had long, worried discussions about whether the lad was going to the dogs. But they seem to have decided that he had a bottom of good sense. He was seeing life—so necessary for writing about it—and he was making contacts. He had become a member of the Unity Club, patronised by actors, publishers, writers and journalists. The Sims's social contacts were wide enough for them to be assured that he was shaping up well in this company.

The word 'Bohemian' to-day has lost its glamour in unwashed coffee cups afloat with disintegrated fag-ends, in dirty fingernails

*George R. Sims, *My Life*, p. 39.

and laddered stockings. But it had a sparkle when Sims was young—
and even when he was old, he subtitled *My Life*, Sixty Years Recollec-
tions of Bohemian London. The Cremorne was an open Bohemian
haunt and Sims did not really make the grade till he became a member
of The Unity Club. There he made friends with people who were to
help him in different sides of his career. George Barrett, the actor, was
the brother of actor–manager Wilson Barrett, who was to stage and
play in many of Sims's plays, starting with the money-spinner *The
Lights o' London*. Andrew (Dan) Chatto was a bright young publisher
working for John Camden Hotten, the bookseller–publisher in
Piccadilly. Dan Chatto took over Hotten's list, after Hotten's death,
and started the firm of Chatto & Windus. He gave Sims his first book
assignment, to translate Balzac's *Contes Drolatiques* which Hotten had
published in French with Doré's illustrations.

Sims was paid £75, insisting on anonymity 'for family reasons' (his
parents' tolerance had its limits). He gladly accepted the commission,
because he was living above his income and his adventures on the
turf didn't recoup his fortunes. The English *Contes Drolatiques*
appeared under the Chatto & Windus imprint but according to Sims
was soon withdrawn for two reasons. (1) A headmaster, beguiled by
the beauty of the volume, bought a number of copies as school prizes,
all—except perhaps one—of which he returned when his wife had
read the work (2) John Ruskin protested that his admiration of the
illustrative talent of Gustave Doré should be advertised as if to
approve this scandalous book.

Sims says the sheets were sold to an American publisher. But in
fact the story is more complicated. There is a Doré edition of Sims's
translation with the imprint of John Camden Hotten; and Sims's own
copy of the translation has no illustrations and is Privately Printed.

Hotten died three years before the English version was first pub-
lished. He was a notorious pirate of American writers, such as Twain,
Harte, Col. John Hay and Ambrose Bierce. Bierce extorted a cheque
for £100 from him on his deathbed, but before cashing it, dropped in
at a pub where suitable epitaphs were being composed, of which the
best was

> Hotten
> Rotten
> Forgotten.

By the time Bierce reached the bank, Hotten's death was known and
his cheque was refused.

Dan Chatto was honourable in paying American royalties, but it seems he used his shady predecessor to push the *Contes Drolatiques*.

The most immediately useful friend that Sims made at the Unity Club was the journalist John Thomson.

Thomson was a lazy man. As dramatic critic of the *Weekly Dispatch,* he was supposed to pass judgement on a play to be revived on a Saturday night. He had seen the play before, so he wrote his critique and went to Brighton for the week-end, only to return and find that the revival had been postponed till Monday.

To Thomson, the eager young Sims, spoiling to write for the newspapers not for money or fame but merely for experience, was a gift from Heaven. Thomson had a weekly chore of grinding out the "Waifs and Strays" column, which had been written by Tom Hood Junior until he became editor of *Fun,* the most vigorous of many rivals to *Punch.* What could be more satisfactory than that George R. Sims should write the copy for the column, while Thomson pocketed the guinea paid for it?

Sims wrote it so capably that after some weeks Thomson gave him the guinea as well. He took the budding journalist under his wing and when Sims showed him a ballad called "Jack's Story", written in the manner of "Jim Bludso" by Colonel John Hay*, Thomson had it set up for the *Weekly Dispatch.* "Jack's Story" was too strong-blooded for Fleet Street in the 1860s, but Ambrose Bierce, the most atrabilious newspaper man ever to dip pen in vitriol, bore it off to California and gave Sims his balladic debut in the *San Francisco News Letter.*

It is probable that Sims gained his *entrée* to the Unity Club by his amiability as a listener and his willingness to stand his round. But he soon established himself as quick, witty, hard-working and sociable. He began a lifelong friendship with Henry Sampson. At that time, Sampson wrote the sports news of the Weekly Dispatch under the Arthurian pseudonym of Pendragon, as well as acting as assistant-editor to Tom Hood.

So when Hood fell ill, Sampson took the editorial chair of *Fun* and invited young Sims to be a contributor of paragraphs and occasional verse.

It had been Sims's boyhood ambition to write for *Fun,* which had on its staff stalwarts like George Augustus Sala and the dramatist Tom Robertson. But when after a few weeks, he was beginning to

*Hay's *Pike County Ballads* had been 'copy-wronged' by Hotten.

feel established, suddenly W. S. Gilbert, an old contributor, re-appeared on the scene. He had quarrelled with the editor of *Punch*, who refused to print "The Yarn of the *Nancy Bell*" because it was "too cannibalistic". Sampson printed it and for some time Gilbert crowded Sims out of *Fun*. It was only when Hood died that Sampson found room for Sims on the staff.

He continued at his father's office. A guinea a week from the *Dispatch* and about £2 a week from *Fun* did not meet the needs of the young Bohemian about town. His day began at 10 am in the City office. 1–2.30 pm visits to editors. 2.30–6 p.m. office and then home. After an hour for dinner, writing until 10.30 or 11 pm; then out to the Unity Club till 3 or 4 am.

In 1877 Sampson left *Fun* to start the Sunday *Referee* primarily a sporting and dramatic paper; George R. Sims went along with him to write a column called 'Mustard and Cress', under the pseudonym of Dagonet, King Arthur's jester.

No feature in late Victorian journalism attracted so intense and personal a following as 'Mustard and Cress'. 'Refereaders', if their copy was not delivered on a Sunday, were known to ring Sims up and ask him to read the week's 'Mustard and Cress' over the telephone, which he obligingly did, leaving suitable pauses for laughter or tears.

I have already described how Dagonet made his Refereaders privy to his home life, his horses, his dogs, his carriage, his favourite restaurants and resorts. He was married twice, his first wife dying tragically young of cancer at the age of thirty-two, his second Florence Wykes, a young actress he had met acting in one of his plays, surviving him by many years. Of them he said little. When Sims wrote *My Life*, there was no mention of them. But in 'Mustard and Cress' there were frequent references to the niece whom he adopted. On the day she was born, Sims remarked that she was 'Dagonet's Mint Sauce for the Lamb'; he suggested she should be christened trebly in his honour Georgina Roberta Dagonetta. When her parents rebelled, Sims just made her 'Minty Lamb'. Refereaders thought he had added a pet sheep to his menagerie until he printed her photograph. Though really Frances Maud Beatrice Wykes, this devoted niece signs her cheques and holds her passport in the name of Minty Lamb, a living Simsian joke.

Dagonet however was no mere gossip columnist. He was interested in everything, in crime and prostitution, the civilising influence of electric street lighting, the necessity of providing costermongers with

G. R. S. and Minty Lamb

stabling so that their wives should not be disturbed by donkeys sleeping under the bed, the working of factory and education acts. Though childless, he became the father-figure of the nation, a good-hearted, generous lover of life, a *bon-viveur,* a race course punter with a flair for the 20 to 1 chance, an incorrigible punster but at the same time champion of the underdog, the overworked or workless, the unjustly accused.

The King of Sweden and Norway made Sims a Knight of the Royal Order of St Olaf for his work in proving the innocence of Adolf Beck. Beck was twice convicted and once condemned to seven years penal servitude for crimes committed by another man. Eric R. Watson[*] seems right that Sims did not announce the innocence of Beck in 1896 (as Sims himself claimed). But Sims was certainly interested in the case by 1901 and had publicly taken up the cause of Beck in May 1903, three months before Beck was arrested by the police on the second false charge. It was due to Sims that Beck received as compensation for his false imprisonment a sum which enabled him to drink himself to death in a few short years. Even more importantly, Sims's agitation headed the outcry for a Royal Commission which tried, but failed, to make this type of false imprisonment impossible in future.

Sims Playwright

If Sims had remained merely newspaperman and columnist, his name would be no more resonant than that of W. T. Stead. He would never have achieved the celebrity of having his wax *doppelgänger* in Madame Tussaud's, if he had not been the most successful English playwright of his age. Of him, Henry Barton Baker might have written as he did of Sims's collaborator, Henry Pettit.

> He was destitute of literary form, his dialogue was utterly commonplace, his characters mere lay figures, but he had a knack of constructing plots out of ancient conventions, of dressing up telling situations, and an unerring eye for stage effect that appealed more strongly to the general public than would any work of genius.[†]

Though Sims could not boast as did an earlier playwright, Edward Stirling, that he had dramatized 247 novels without permission or

---

[*]Eric R. Watson, *Adolf Beck* (Notable Trial Series).
[†]*History of the London Stage and its Famous Players (1576–1903)* Routledge 1904, Vol 2. p. 436.

payment, the number of plays from the continent which he took and made over to the English taste, either alone or with collaborators, ran into dozens. He received these assignments as a result of a satirical play of his own, *Crutch and Toothpick,* which made a modest success. The financial rewards were small, either an outright payment or a fixed performance fee. Though he churned out these adaptations at the rate of one a month, besides contributing regularly to three weekly newspapers, he fell into debt and borrowed £1,000 from money-lenders at the iniquitous interest of sixty per cent p.a.

It was not until the production in September 1881 of his second original, a melodrama entitled *The Lights o' London,* that his financial position was assured. The play had been on the stocks for years without any manager being prepared to launch it. The story of its being written is interesting.

Sims was a great walker and, in his own words,

> One afternoon when walking from St Albans to London, near Barnet I fell in with a young fellow and his wife. They seemed decent folk. The man told me he was tramping to London in search of work.
>
> . . . as we came to Highgate the lights of the City were just visible in the rather misty darkness.
>
> 'Look, Liz,' exclaimed the man eagerly to his wife as he stretched out his hand towards the City paved with gold. 'Yonder are the lights o' London.'

That night Sims wrote

THE LIGHTS
OF LONDON TOWN

The way was long and weary,
  But gallantly they strode,
A country lad and lassie,
  Along the heavy road.
The night was dark and stormy,
  But blithe of heart were they,
For shining in the distance
  The lights of London lay.
O gleaming lamps of London that gem the city's crown,
What fortunes lie within you, O Lights of London Town!

PREPARE TO SHED THEM NOW

The years passed on and found them
　　Within the mighty fold,
The years had brought them trouble,
　　But brought them little gold,
Oft from their garret window,
　　On long, still, summer nights,
They'd seek the far-off country
　　Beyond the London lights.
O mocking lamps of London, what weary eyes look down,
And mourn the day they saw you, O Lights of London Town!

With faces worn and weary,
　　That told of sorrow's load,
One day a man and woman
　　Crept down a country road.
They sought their native village,
　　Heart-broken from the fray,
Yet shining still behind them,
　　The lights of London lay.
O cruel lamps of London, if tears your light could drown,
Your victims' eyes would weep them, O Lights of London Town!

Dickens in *Bleak House* had already described countrymen plod-
ding to London from St Albans in search of work. But in the 1870s,
the experience was still common enough to strike a chord in people's
hearts. Set to music by Louis Diehl, the song proved so popular that
Sims decided to make it the theme for a play in five acts.

The opening of Act One at the Seat of Squire Armytage gives the
flavour.

As the curtain rises SQUIRE ARMYTAGE is discovered seated beneath
tree C. He leans on stick. Marks, the lodge-keeper, stands respectfully
L.C.

SQUIRE *(R.C. on seat under tree)* Three years—three years to-day since he
　　stood here, as you stand now, Marks, and I told him to go, for
　　he was no longer a son of mine!

MARKS I sometimes think you might have given Master Harold another
　　chance, Squire.

SQUIRE *(rises)* I bore with him until I could bear no longer—till the tales

18

of his wild ways came down here and were village gossip—Then
I bade him see my face no more, and he went!

MARKS   Yes, he went out through your gates—a beggar!

SQUIRE   And from that day you have never seen your daughter?

MARKS   No—She's written me now and again to say she was well in
London.

SQUIRE   She went with him! He crowned his wickedness by enticing your
child to share his vagabond life!

When Wilson Barrett accepted *The Lights o' London* for The Princess's Theatre, Haymarket, Sims suggested a downright payment of £500 and was going on to name a small performance fee. Barrett refused. He offered for West End performances

2 guineas, if takings were under £600

5   per cent of box-office when takings were from £600–£700

$7\frac{1}{2}$ per cent of box-office when takings were from £700–£800

10   per cent of box-office when takings were above £800.

Provincial rates were on a similar, but lower, sliding scale.

The Lights o' London ran for 228 performances at the Princess's and in *My Life* Sims himself claimed that it had been played somewhere on the face of the earth ever since that first September evening thirty-five years before. When the New York *Sunday Advertiser* reckoned in 1894 Sims had already made £72,000 out of *The Lights o' London,* the figure was probably as unreliable as all those in show-biz. But from 1881 onwards Sims no longer had to worry about money or money-lenders.

Dudley Cook*, a contemporary critic, ascribed the popular appeal of the play to the fact that a street in Hoxton, dreary in life, became exciting transferred to the stage. The first act was slow and common-place. One knew that everything would come right in the end. But good comedy scenes and a skilful introduction of new themes kept interest alive. And it was refreshing to see old familiar players in new disguises.

In the chorus of praise, it was probably only Sims himself who heard the still small voice of William Archer murmuring 'Zola diluted at Aldgate Pump.'

---

* *Nights at the Play,* vol. 3, p. 333/5.

PREPARE TO SHED THEM NOW

Novelist and Short Storywriter

As if one play a month and three articles a week was not enough, the indefatigable Sims produced novels and short story collections which with his splendid sense of continuity he published with Chatto & Windus. Oliver Warner, too young himself ever to have met Sims, has reminiscences of the conversation of the Chatto manager George Frommholz 'now with God, lucky old God'. 'Ah, Mr Warner, George R. Sims, *he* was the boy! used to turn up just before the partners went out to lunch. Used to say he could smell the roast beef all the way down St. Martin's Lane.'

The partners were Andrew Chatto and Percy Spalding, and I wrote to Frank Swinnerton, in his youth a reader for Chatto and still with us, lucky old us. 'As a youth I caught sight of him once or twice at Chatto & Windus,' Swinnerton replied by return of post, 'a very plump man, under middle height, with the luxurious beard one saw in photographs: but never spoke, and knew nothing about him. All I remember is that when I was begging the firm might take the offered chance of publishing Constance Garnett's translation of Tchekov's Tales, which Heinemann had turned down, Mr Spalding, the senior partner, hummed: 'Hm, short stories. We didn't do very well with that last book of Sims's short stories.'

That was in the 1900s, but for many years before then Chatto's had done well with Sims's collections of short stories, originally published in newspapers, often at Christmas. (For every thousand people who know 'Christmas Day in the Workhouse' is there one who knows his short story 'Christmas Day in a Coal-hole?')

Sims's short stories have an improbability as audacious as that of his plays and ballads, but the more glaring because they can be pondered. My favourite is 'The Ring o' Bells'.

On Christmas Eve Mr Sparkins is giving his annual rendering of 'The Mistletoe Bough' in The Ring o' Bells, Marshton-by-the-sea, kept by widow Van Hooten. In comes a young woman and swoons. Having given birth to a baby girl, she dies. The widow keeps the child, whom she calls Mary Holland. But she treats the child harshly. She also treats Mr Sparkins harshly, refusing to marry him after a delicate courtship of seven years. In retaliation Mr Sparkins refuses to sing 'The Mistletoe Bough'.

There is gloom in the Ring o' Bells next Christmas, because no 'Mistletoe Bough', when suddenly comes a sweet voice singing to a violin outside the pub. The song? 'The Mistletoe Bough'!

Poor little Mary, the drudge, is sent into the snow to fetch the strangers in, but she can't find them, until she comes to Mr Sparkins's house, having prayed 'Oh, mother, dear mother! ask God to let me find the musicians and take them back with me.'

Learning her quest, Mr Sparkins remarks with a malignant grin: 'Ho, ho! that's it, is it . . . she wants them back in my place, does she? Ho, ho! Then you go back, my dear, and tell her she won't have 'em.'

Then taking pity on Mary's fright, he invites her in for a piece of cake and she meets the blind fiddler and the boy singer who is his 'eyes'.

The man took up his old violin, and presently it seemed to those who listened that the voices of the angels were filling the room with song. In all the years that he had been parish clerk, Mr Sparkins had never heard such music. The man himself forgot his listeners, and played on in a kind of ecstasy. His face seemed transfigured. Suddenly the angels' chorus ceased, and from the strings of the old violin there came a plaintive ballad of human love—a woman's gentle voice sang tearfully of happier days. Softer and softer the music grew, until it seemed to the enraptured listeners that the voice was borne away from earth to heaven, and then, as it died away and was lost in the far-off clouds, there was a low sob and silence.

Mr Sparkins opened his eyes with a start. The sob was so real. It couldn't be the fiddle. No fiddle ever sobbed like that. It was not the fiddle, but the fiddler. The sob was his—the violin had dropped from his hand and rested between his knees, and his cheeks, browned with sun, wind, and travel, were wet with the salt drops that trickled slowly down them.

. . . When the last sob had died away, and the player's head was bowed in grief, the child, not knowing what she did, stole up to him and put her arms about his neck, and touched his cheek with her lips.

'It is the angels' song that you have played, sir, is it not?' she whispered.

'Yes, little one,' said the man, slowly raising his head. 'It is the angels' song. It is the song of one who was the angel of my life.'

'Ah, I know,' cried the child; 'it is the song my mother sings.'

The man started. 'Your mother, child—your mother sings that song? You have heard that music before?'

'No,' answered the child, 'I have not heard it; but if it's the angels' song, it is my mother's, for she is with the angels now.'

This is not the climax of the story, which meanders across revolutionary Europe before Mary finds that the blind man is her father and they retire to London to live on the profits of the Ring o' Bells, managed for them by Mr Sparkins. The plot is one of melodramatic tidiness. But the passage I have quoted is interesting as an early example of a cross-fertilisation with which we are familiar to-day. Many modern novels are drawn not from life, but from the cinema. As we read, we think not 'This is true' but 'This would make a good film.' So the reader of Mary, the blind fiddler and the angels' song must have murmured, 'What a beautiful magic lantern slide that would make!'

The Social Reporter

In 1882/3 George R. Sims wrote two series of articles which roused the conscience of the nation, provoked a Royal Commission and shook the complacence of many legislators and administrators who thought people could be managed like things. The first, *How the Poor Live,* was written for the *Pictorial World*. Its sequel *Horrible London* appeared in the *Daily News*. In the foreword to the 1889 edition of the two collected series, published by Chatto & Windus, Sims wrote:

> If an occasional lightness of treatment seems to the reader out of harmony with so grave a subject, I pray that he will remember the work was undertaken to enlist the sympathies of a class not generally given to the study of low life.

Whereas Friedrich Engels sought support for revolutionary theory in his pamphlet *Conditions of the Working Class in 1844*, while the brothers Mayhew had explored the conditions of the London working classes extensively and in detail and Charles Booth had given a lifetime to the study of the *Occupations of the people, 1841–81*, George R. Sims set himself a humbler but not less urgent task. He aimed to teach the well-to-do how the poor lived and convince them that, if only for selfish reasons, they should do something to make conditions better. His use of the *argumentum ad hominem* was brilliant. Even the silliest middle-class mother could grasp that measles, small-pox and scarlet fever were no respecters of social classes. He was prepared to face his readers with shocking material, like his quotations from the reports of Mr Wrack, a local government inspector. Here is one of them.

INTRODUCTION

PROLONGED RETENTION OF A DEAD BODY
IN A ROOM OCCUPIED BY A FAMILY

Mr Wrack reports that, on visiting No 17 Hope Street, Spitalfields, he found in the room on the second floor the dead body of a child who had died fifteen days before the time of his visit. The room, which contained 1,176 cubic feet of space, was occupied by the parents of the dead child and a daughter aged thirteen years. The body was in a decomposed state. The reason assigned for not burying the child at an earlier period was that the father had no means to do so, and that his friends had failed to render him the assistance which they had promised. Mr Wrack having pointed out the danger of keeping a dead body so long in the only room occupied by the family, application was made to the relieving officer, and the body was removed on the following day.

Such a tale might horrify his readers, but to drive their danger home, he followed it with a slightly different story. On a table lay the uncoffined body of a child who had died of scarlet fever. Five people lived and slept in that room, of whom the four adults worked there, tailoring for folks who might be immune to social conscience but were not immune to scarlet fever carried by the garments tailored.

In none of the quoted cases of 'Prolonged Detention of Dead Bodies' could the corpse be removed to the public mortuary, because there was none. And the Home Secretary, when his notice was called to this, merely replied 'he would be glad to introduce Bills upon this and many other subjects, but there was no time for them.'

The contrasts of 19th century London were violent. Within a hundred yards of Drury Lane Theatre were slums so noisome that their overcrowded population died of 'exhalations'. To get into these slum rooms, Sims did not dress down as Jack London did to get the material for *The People of the Abyss*. He was sometimes mistaken for a plain clothes detective; but when his identity was disclosed as 'Geeuss' Sims, the author of the Dagonet Ballads, the poet of the poor, he was welcomed. It was only natural that afterwards, to get the stench of these places out of his nostrils, he should call in at Romano's or Gatti's or one of his clubs, The Green Room or The Devonshire.

In *Sybil* Disraeli had described the British as belonging to Two Nations. George R. Sims held dual citizenship. Without a mellowing of claret, he might have made his articles too harsh. Without reimmersion in the lower depths, he would have grown smug. Balanced between these poles, he believed it enough to leave the world a little better than he found it. Not for him Utopia to-morrow or next century. It was enough to gentle progress by bringing a tear to the eye, a laugh to the throat, a righteous quickening to the pulse.

To the squalor of conditions, he added the pathos of the poor and the vigour of their young; and he was no friend of do-gooders who condemned the few pleasures which made slumdom tolerable.

Many people object to the music-halls as sinks of iniquity. That they are unmixed blessings I am not going to contend, but if properly conducted they do an immense amount of comparative good. Drink is sold certainly in some of them, but few people get drunk. A very little liquor goes a long way at a hall, and the people, being amused and interested in the entertainment, do not want much liquid sustenance. . . . In the East End of London there are several places where a big entertainment is given and no liquor is sold at all. At one of them—the best of its kind in London—there are two houses nightly. From seven till nine dramas are performed, then everybody is turned out and the house is refilled with a fresh audience for a music-hall entertainment—and nearly every evening the theatre is crammed to suffocation; the admission is 1*d* the gallery, 2*d* the pit, and 3*d* and 6*d* the upper circle and boxes. On the night of our visit there wasn't room to cram another boy in the place; the gallery and pit were full of boys and girls of from eight to fifteen, I should say, and the bulk of the audience in the other parts were quite young people.

The gallery was a sight which, once seen, could never be forgotten. It was one dense mass of little faces and white bare arms twined and intertwined like snakes round a tree—tier above tier of boys rising right away from the front rows until the heads of the last row touched the ceiling. It was a jam—not a crowd—when one boy coughed it shook the thousands wedged in and round about; and when one boy got up to go out he had to crawl and walk over the heads of the others; space below for a human foot to rest there was absolutely none.

All this vast audience was purely local. Our advent, though our attire was a special get-up for the occasion, attracted instant attention, and the cry of 'Hottentots' went round. 'Hottentots' is the playful way in this district of designating a stranger, that is to say, a stranger come from the West.

The entertainment was admirable; the artists were clever, and in only one case absolutely vulgar; and the choruses were joined in by the entire assembled multitude.

When it was time for the chorus to leave off and the singer to go on again, an official in uniform, standing by the orchestra, and commanding the entire house, raised his hand, and instantly, as if by magic, the chorus ceased.

A sketch like this was immensely reassuring to the well-to-do who in those days viewed the poor rather as Afrikaners view Africans and Coloureds to-day, as creatures belonging to a different species of creation. Sims's instinct for persuasion was subtle. Humanitarianism was not enough. There were many possible ways of denouncing bad working conditions. Sims chose one which would strike at its most sentimental moment.

> The work which these girls have to do in return for a small wage is generally of a dangerous character. Many of them literally snatch their food from the jaws of death.
>
> One girl in the Home was white and ill and weak, and her story may be taken as a sample. She worked at the 'bronzing,' that is, a branch of the chromo-lithography business, and it consists in applying a fluid, which gives off a poisonous exhalation, to certain work. Bronzing enters largely into the composition of those Christmas pictures which delight us so much at the festive season, and which adorn the nursery of many a happy, rosy-cheeked English child.
>
> The law, recognising the dangerous nature of the work, says that the girls doing it shall be allowed a pint of milk per day, the milk in some way counteracting the effect of the poison the girls inhale. It will hardly be believed that some of the best firms refuse to comply with the regulation, and if the girls complain they are at once discharged.
>
> Now, the wages paid are seven shillings per week. To keep at their employment it is necessary that the workers take castor-oil daily, and drink at least a pint of milk. They must either pay for these luxuries out of their scanty earnings or go without, and eventually find their way to hospital.

Christmas Cards at that time were not thrown in the dustbin or put aside for a Cheshire Home to be made over for another year. They were pasted in albums to beguile the long winter evenings. Sims knew that for thousands looking at pretty chromo-lithographs, the pleasure would be marred by the thought of the girls who snatched 'their food from the jaws of death'. The pictures on the nursery wall would be framed reminders.

He was equally back-handed in his description of over-crowding.

. . . I may as well quote an instance which bears directly upon the interest —the selfish interest—which the better classes have in lending their voices to swell the chorus of complaints which is going up about the present state of things.

Here is an 'interior' to which I would call the special attention of ladies who employ nurse-girls for their children.

This room when we entered it was in a condition beyond description. The lady was washing the baby, and she made that the excuse for the dirt of everything else. Two ragged boys were sitting on the filthy floor, a dirty little girl was in a corner pulling a dirty kitten's tail, and the smoke from the untidiest grate I ever saw in my life was making the half-washed baby sneeze its little head nearly off. The family, all told, that slept in this room was seven. There was a bed and there was a sofa—so I concluded the floor must have been the resting-place for some of them. 'The eldest girl'—the materfamilas informed us in answer to our questions—'was gone out. She slept on the sofa.' We knew somebody had slept there, because some rags were on it, which had evidently done duty as bed-clothes.

Outside this room, which opened on to a back-yard, was a dust-bin. We didn't want eyesight to know that—it appealed with sufficient power to another sense. Inside was an odour which made the dust-bin rather a relief.

I have described this place a little graphically for the sake of that eldest girl. It is not from any gallantry to the fair sex that I have done this, but because the young woman in question was, I ascertained, a domestic servant. She was a nursemaid just home from a place at Norwood, and in a week she was going to a place at Clapham.

Now, if you will take the trouble to think out the possible result of girls going from such pigsties as these straight into well-to-do families, where they will nurse the children and be constantly in closest contact with the younger members of the family, I think you will see that the dangers of unhealthy homes for the poor may be equally dangerous to a better class. I should like to know how many families now mourning the loss of a little child from fever, or the death of some dear one from small-pox, would have been spared their sorrow had the existence of such places as I have described been rendered impossible by the action of the law!

Politics is the art of the possible. Perhaps that is why Sims did not set his sights high. The complete solution of slum problems was impossible in his time; and if he had demanded too much, his readers would have thrown up their hands in despair. And so would he.

Sims saw the time as one for sharp decision, as in a ship sinking without enough boats and life-buoys. The only thing was to save the best and let the others drown. The unsavable were criminals, alcoholics, drug-addicts, the old, the subnormal, ignorant and improvident. He was ruthless by modern standards, but in his time he was right. With limited resources, you can help most those who have some capacity to help themselves. So he advocated the separation of the sheep from the goats.

Housing schemes, then as to-day, tore down the houses of the very poor and replaced them with houses for the not-so-poor. Sims wanted cheap houses for the deserving poor near their work, and built for the needs of their trades (e.g. stables for costermongers). It was ridiculous to house dockers miles from the docks. The important thing was to prevent the children of dockers and costermongers growing up in the same houses as thieves, prostitutes and ponces.

He believed that Board School Education drew a line between the past and the present. The Education Acts were creating a new generation. But education was not free. Unless poverty could be pleaded to the remission board, 2d a week was levied for each child, a heavy burden on many families. School meals were not provided. Several newspapers collected funds to provide slum children with Christmas Dinners. Dagonet, more wisely, supported a scheme to provide London Board School children with school meals during the winter. Here are four cases he quotes as coming before the remission board. They throw a light on the background of his Ballads.

1. Mrs Walker. Seven children of school age; fee 2d a week each. Total earnings of entire family, 10s. Rent, 5s 6d. Husband once good mechanic, lost employment through illness and deafness. Parish relief none. Character good. Is now a hawker—sells oranges and fish. Children half-starved. When an orange is too bad to sell they have it for breakfast, with a piece of bread.

2. Mr Thompson. Five children of school age. Out of work. No income but pawning clothes and goods. Rent, 4s. Wife drinks surreptitiously. Husband, good character.

3. Mrs ——. Five children of school age; widow. Earnings 6s. Rent, 3s. Her husband when alive was a Drury Lane clown. Respectable woman; feels her poverty very keenly.

4.   Mr Garrad. Eight children of school age; two always under doctor. No income. Pawning last rags. Rent, 5s 6d. No parish relief. Starving. Declines to go into workhouse.

The Elementary Education Acts bore most hardly on those least able to profit. Bright children passed out at eleven and began to earn. Backward children, usually from poorer homes where money was more needed, could be held at school until fourteen to meet the grade.

In one school, Sims found a child 'but one remove from an idiot — the offspring of a gentleman whose present address is Holloway Gaol, and a lady who has been charged seventy-three times with being drunk and incapable. . . . The child has just sufficient intelligence to escape the asylum, and between the asylum and the school there is no half-way house.'

Sitting next to this sub-normal child was a girl of nine whose story might well have become a Simsian Ballad. Her father was a boatman. When his wife asked him for the remains of his wages after he came home from the pub, he struck her with a boat-hook and injured her brain. She was committed to an insane asylum.

When he sobered up, the father fled, leaving his daughter an 'orphan with living parents'. The child was taken in by her grand-mother.

One day this year the old lady passed some men carrying a body found in the river to the dead-house. Curiosity induced her to go in with the crowd, and the face of the dead man was that of her son.

Sims heard this story from the little girl's teacher, in front of the child, a model pupil whose intelligence was heightened by the dark-ness of the moron beside her.

'And your granny keeps you now?' says the teacher, as she concludes the little history and turns to the girl.
   'Yes, teacher; and when I grow up, I'm going to keep granny.'
   So may it be!

The idioms of devotion change. No child, even in a work of devo-tional fiction, if such are now written, could express herself thus to-day; and if a modern novelist dared to describe this scene he would use it as a prologue to a tale of hideous sterility, the dedication to Granny of a spinster growing sour in menopause.

But this was how the poor lived in the 1880s.

It provides a clue to how the Dagonet and other Ballads were written in the 1870s and 1880s and to their popularity among different classes in the decades that followed.

Sims, the Balladist

Sims, as I have said, was not an originator but an adaptor. Though the field of his Ballads was English, the formula was American, taken from the *Pike County Ballads* of Colonel John Hay. It was a simple recipe. In colloquial language and heavily accented verse, a first person narrator told a melodramatic story, expressing often opinions which appeared almost blasphemous but which in fact robustly restated simple faith.

Since Colonel John Hay's two most famous ballads, 'Little Breeches' and 'Jim Bludso of the Prairie Belle' have recently been reprinted*, let me quote another gem.

BANTY TIM

Remarks of Sergeant Tilmon Joy to the
White Man's Committee of Spunky Point, Illinois

I reckon I git your drift, gents,—
　　You 'low the boy sha'n't stay;
This is a white man's country;
　　You're Dimocrats, you say;
And whereas, and seein', and wherefore,
　　The times bein' all out o' j'int,
The nigger has got to mosey
　　From the limits o' Spunky P'int!

---

* *Parlour Poetry,* Michael R. Turner, Michael Joseph, 1967.

Le's reason the thing a minute:
    I'm an old-fashioned Dimocrat too,
Though I laid my politics out o' the way
    For to keep till the war was through.
But I come back here, allowin'
    To vote as I used to do,
Though it gravels me like the devil to train
    Along o' sich fools as you.

Now dog my cats ef I kin see,
    In all the light of the day,
What you've got to do with the question
    Ef Tim shill go or stay.
And furder than that I give notice,
    Ef one of you tetches the boy,
He kin check his trunks to a warmer clime
    Than he'll find in Illanoy.

Why, blame your hearts, jest hear me!
    You know that ungodly day
When our left struck Vicksburg Heights, how ripped
    And torn and tattered we lay.
When the rest retreated I stayed behind,
    Fur reasons sufficient to me,—
With a rib caved in, and a leg on a strike,
    I sprawled on that damned glacee.

Lord! how the hot sun went for us,
    And br'iled and blistered and burned!
How the rebel bullets whizzed round us
    When a cuss in his death-grip turned!
Till along toward dusk I seen a thing
    I could n't believe for a spell:
That nigger—that Tim—was a crawlin' to me
    Through that fire-proof, gilt-edged hell!

The Rebels seen him as quick as me,
    And the bullets buzzed like bees;
But he jumped for me, and he shouldered me,
    Though a shot brought him once to his knees;
But he staggered up, and packed me off,
    With a dozen stumbles and falls,
Till safe in our lines he drapped us both,
    His black hide riddled with balls

So, my gentle gazelles, thar's my answer,
    And here stays Banty Tim:
He trumped Death's ace for me that day,
    And I'm not going back on him!
You may rezoloot till the cows come home,
    But ef one of you tetches the boy,
He'll wrastle his hash to-night in hell,
    Or my name's not Tilmon Joy!

The occasions of war change. Then it was the American Civil War; now it is the war in Vietnam. Though no popular poet would speak of black hides being 'riddled with balls' in this outspoken age, the sentiment of comradeship in arms transcending colour difference is as powerful to-day as it was a century ago. Banty Tim is crude; but melodrama has not aged to comedy.

Like Bret Harte and Mark Twain, Colonel John Hay was a highly literate man, using slang in order to escape from literary clichés. It was an attempt to salvage something from 'The Wreck of the Hesperus.' Reciters were tiring of Longfellow's insipidity.

It was the schooner Hesperus,
    That sailed the wintry sea;
And the skipper had taken his little daughter
    To bear him company.

But they were not ready for Gerard Manley Hopkins's 'The Wreck of the Deutschland'.

John Hay, a lawyer who became Secretary and Aide-de-Camp to President Lincoln, Ambassador to England and Secretary of State, was a conscious exploiter of The Vernacular Fallacy.

Mr. Sims's Birthday Tea

'Flush'.   *'Barney Barnato'*

G. R. S. at Work

Christmas Day in the Workhouse

It is true that popular ballads, evolved in saloons and round camp-fires, have a beauty and directness which comes from the struggle between force of meaning and weakness of vocabulary, the poetry of common speech. The Vernacular Fallacy arises when the literate culti-vate illiteracy. Theirs are cultured, not real, pearls of speech. 'Who is it works for Art's sake?' asked Sims. 'I want to go down well with people who buy papers, see plays, and read books at the present day.' He had enormous facility. He was not cynical about anything except Art for Art's sake. Though he wrote much purely to give people pleasure—which is not so disreputable as it is regarded by some writers whose integrity demands that they should write purely to give people pain—Sims was a sincere radical, a non-Puritanical reformer interested in the problems of his day, sanitation, slum-clearance, employment, poor-relief and education.

He took Colonel John Hay's ballad form and adapted it to his own uses. As he said in *My Life,* he never regarded his ballads as poetry. They were recitation pieces.

To-day, despite the flood of radio and television entertainment, spoken poetry is more popular than it has been since 1914. Young people spend evenings reading poetry to one another. The Albert Hall is hired for poetic happenings and all over the place, in small gatherings, poets meet to read their poems to or at audiences.

But this revival of spoken poetry is very different, from the Vic-torian entertainment, so well celebrated by J. B. Preistley in nostalgic mood. Entertainment was made in home and church hall, by amateur musicians and reciters. Recitation was the refuge of those who could not sing or play a musical instrument; and in the rendering of humour, pathos, nobility, resignation etc as much agony was endured by those performing as by those performed against.

These recitations were done not merely by amateurs. Sims relates that Herbert Beerbohm Tree made one of his first successes by reciting 'Told to the Missionary' one of the 'Dagonet Ballads'. Tree, later to become Sir Herbert, showed false nicety in altering to 'dog' the key shock-word 'bitch'.

'Told to a Missionary', printed on p. 100, is a splendid example of the vernacular method. A dying costermonger is being entreated by the conventionally 'unco guid' missionary to 'think on Jesus'. Though the missionary doesn't get a word in edgewise, we get a good idea of what he's like by his fear of the old bitch. But since the coster is a rough sort of chap, we don't at first know whether the old bitch is a dog or his wife. Then having discovered that she is a real and not colloquial bitch, we are faced with the even more challenging idea that the bitch and Jesus Christ have a lot in common.

'Told to the Missionary' first appeared in the *Referee,* like the even more famous 'In the Workhouse: Christmas Day' and 'Billy's Rose'. They were reprinted in his first collection *The Dagonet Ballads,* which consisted of 16 dramatic ballads and 9 pieces of occasional verse. They achieved such success that the paperback edition alone, price sixpence, post free seven stamps, had sold a hundred thousand copies by 1879.

Highbrow critics might dismiss his ballads as 'twaddle', but in the course of a long review of the second collection *Ballads of Babylon* the *Daily Telegraph* wrote

> It is apparently the literary mission of Mr Sims to do in verse what Dickens did in prose, and to bind all classes of his fellow-citizens together with the bonds of sympathy. He carries us with him into the cellars of the slums, and draws for us unbeautiful, unromantic men and women and children, whom he makes to seem beautiful with the often unseen light of love and tenderness. His charity, born of a fine insight into the workings of the mind, casts a halo of unlooked for sweetness around the lives of vagabonds and outcasts. . . . There is about his narrative poems of the poor a truth to nature and a facility of expression which betoken a real touch of genius . . . Mr Sims deals with the criminal and horrible side of London life in the plain language and the uncompromising literary spirit of a Zola; with this difference, however, that while the French apostle of a degraded realism wallows in the most revolting details of his subject, and lectures on social disease and preventible vice with the cold exactness of a demonstrator of anatomy explaining the human skeleton, Mr Sims never for one moment loses sight of the moral aspects of his studies.

Surveying the 'Literature of 1880', Robert Buchanan, himself a popular poet, went even further in the *Contemporary Review.*

> To our mind, at least, a poem such as 'Billy's Rose' is worth a whole heca- tomb of more pretentious verse. In the course of two modest little volumes Mr Sims finds his poetic materials among squalid alleys, filthy lanes, and sunless habitations; he selects coarse elements and shrinks from no reality; and although he does not talk rubbish about 'the terrible Balzac' and 'Shelley, poet of poets, and purest of men.' He is, in a word, an authentic poet, none the less sure of recognition because he does not care to pose as a genius, or because he has shown no super-agile anxiety to be

'discovered'. . . . What Bret Harte did for the American backwoods he is doing for London and its slums, showing how much golden sincerity and pearl-white self-sacrifice may exist in the very dregs of the social deposits; and his task is the more terrible, while his triumph is surely the greater, seeing that, unlike the American writer, he is dealing with themes and persons so ugly and unpoetical in themselves. Many of his ballads are perfect of their kind; all are finely human, and most are deeply pathetic. . . . Mr Tennyson has also recently published ballads. . . . It is not going too far, however, to say that, in the domain of town life and pathetic 'human' writing, Mr Sims does not suffer by comparison even with the laureate.

It is often the fate of the pathos of yesterday to become the bathos of today. But the reasons for Sims's instant success with the *Daily Telegraph* and the *Contemporary Review* critics are worth examining. They are social rather than literary.

The Two Nations of which Benjamin Disraeli had written in *Sybil*, published a couple of years before George R. Sims was born, were as distinct and separate in the 1870s and 80s when Sims wrote his Ballads. Though Trollope might distinguish the niceties of classes, which cut those whose wealth was gained from commerce off from the nobility and landed gentry, these distinctions were as nothing compared with the chasm between the poor and the well-to-do.

These two nations were not comfortably separated geographically. The foulest slums existed down side-alleys off the finest streets. Indeed the poor and rich lived together in the same houses, slaveys working in dark basements and sleeping in cold and draughty attics beneath the slates, while, on the floors between, the master and his family lived in comparative luxury and ease.

This produced an ambivalence in both the nations, but especially in the well-to-do, living in the cosier state 'in which it had pleased God to call them'. Strictness must be tempered with mercy provided that it was not necessary, in order to preserve law, order and property, that mercy should be tempered with strictness. The well-to-do could not afford to regard all the poor as human beings for whom they were morally responsible. There were too many of them. Charity must be confined to the 'deserving poor', if not to unlucky fall-outs from the well-to-do, such as 'Distressed Gentlewomen'.

Auden has described ours as The Age of Anxiety; but if Anxiety means unconscious guilt, the description was more applicable to the Victorian. How to make of the Two Nations one nation? How to recognise the common humanity of two breeds existing side by side in the streets, but never meeting in equality except as the animal with two backs?

The poor were dirty, ignorant, foul-mouthed, drunken and far too numerous. In the house, the shop or factory they could be kept under control. But in the dark streets of the slums they were menacing. The spectre of bloody revolution lurked in the wings of the Victorian scene and just beyond the limelight milled the anonymous unknown and unknowable masses. This terrifying force, like that of sex, was little spoken of; and for that reason more disturbing.

The instant success of Dickens owed less perhaps to his genius than to his ability to adventure into darkest England and survive to bring back to the well-to-do tidings of its benighted inhabitants. At home he was as heroic a character as Dr Livingstone in Africa, whose exploits prompted the uneasy religious to support foreign missions to the heathen.

Dickens, of course, was not alone; but he was less angry, less revolutionary, than Marx and Engels. Changes of heart and law, he believed, could accomplish more than the overthrow of governments. His villains were abusers of functions which could be exercised con-structively with good will, intelligence and unselfishness. Money power might be bad in the hands of Ralph Nickleby, but it was good in the hands of the brothers Cheeryble. Bumbledom, Dotheboys Hall, the Court of Chancery were scandals, but they did not invalidate good administration, education or the principles of justice. Dickens could provoke sympathy for his victims, whatever their class, because he provided the villains whom the reader could blame and thus be purged of any personal sense of guilt.

The comparison between the novels of Charles Dickens and the ballads of George R. Sims was based on their similar social role. The Simsian ballad employed the Dickensian formula for catharsis. Take the example of 'In the Workhouse: Christmas Day'. The well-to-do readers, or audience, might not immediately identify themselves with the paupers sitting at their tables. But they dissociated themselves from the 'guardians and their ladies' who had come in their furs and wrappers 'to be hosts at the workhouse banquet they've paid for— with the rates.'

In the third verse, the meek and lowly paupers were reintroduced with their ' "Thank 'ee kindly, mum's"/So long as they fill their stomachs, what matter it whence it comes?' This produced a clever non-identification with the meek and lowly and a readiness to accept as spokesman the old man who cried, 'Great God! but it chokes me!'

From this point on, identification was complete. If to-day the death of the wife while her husband is snatching a crust from a dog appears melodramatic, is it more so than the Irish family, quoted by Sims who went on tailoring to earn money for the coffin and funeral of a child dead from scarlet fever?

In my childhood people who had no wit tried to raise laughs by saying things like 'Squattez vous' or 'Christmas Day in the Workhouse.' Bawdified versions of the ballad were recited at smoking concerts and parodies in the music halls. But the photograph (p. 33) of dinner at a workhouse represents a scene twenty years after Sims wrote his ballad. 'Vastly as it has been improved of late years,' wrote W. T. Wilkinson, of this reformed workhouse 'it can be still further bettered without putting a premium on laziness.'* One can see that.

The best parody of the Ballads was produced by George Grossmith, an old friend who applied the Dagonet treatment to Eliza Cook's famous recitation piece 'The Old Armchair'.

BROKERS AHEAD!
or the OLD ARM CHAIR

I was seated alone in my room, lads,
    And a knock there came at the door,
I answered the knock myself, lads;
    I'd no servant, for I was poor.

I was overwhelmed with grief, lads,
    And was wretched and low and sad,
For I had a habit of spending
    A good deal more than I had.

I know it was wrong to do so,
    And my fault I freely confess;
But when you've nothing a year, lads,
    You can't very well spend less.

*Living London, ed. G. R. Sims, Vol II, Sec. 1. p. 106, 1906.

INTRODUCTION

When two men entered the room, lads,
  My heart was faint and sick,
For I knew they were both of them brokers
  Who had come for every stick.

The water and gas had been cut off,
  A hard enough blow, lads, was that;
But they wanted to seize the old arm-chair
  In which my great grandmother sat.

It wasn't a chair much to look at,
  With age it was dingy and brown,
And its legs would often give way, lads,
  And would sometimes let people down.

But 'twas seized by the heartless brokers,
  Who carried it off with a jeer,
And my heart was like that of a baby's,
  And my eyes were dimmed with a tear.

Then they went to the little wine cupboard—
  A bottle there stood on the shelf;
They seized it but found it was empty,
  I'd finished that bottle myself.

And they seized all my shirts and my collars,
  Of the latter I had but a few;
And they pounced on my only sheet, lads,
  Which had served as a table-cloth, too.

When they stripped me of every stick, lads,
  Another knock came at the door,
And I answered the knock myself, lads,
  As I'd no servant, for I was poor.

But I found 'twas the family lawyer
  Who said a relation had died,
And, believe me, I danced with delight, lads,
  And I laughed, and I laughed till I cried.

My heart was like that of a schoolboy's,
    You could hear its beats and its bounds,
For I knew that that good old relation
    Had left me a million pounds.

The brokers brought back every stick, lads,
    I paid them their claim and they fled,
And the arm-chair and I both gave way, lads,
    And I fractured the back of my head.

I am now worth a million of money,
    I owe not a penny, I swear;
And if ever I get into debt, lads,
    You may sit on the old arm-chair.

Parody is a form of tribute and Grossmith presented Sims with a copy of his programme, which the latter treasured. It did not mean that Grossmith thought less of the Ballads than he did of Sir Henry Irving, whom he impersonated giving a toast to the health of Mr Beerbohm Tree and the latter's response. In fact you only parody what commands respect.

To us most of the ballads here reprinted are extravagantly funny. It seems impossible to believe that Sims was regarded as one of the immortals; until one reads the roster of the Victorian Parnassus 'Burns, Hood, Wordsworth, Mackay, Swain, Longfellow, Whittier, Lowell, Carleton, Felicia Hemans and Letitia E. Landon.' The comedy of the Dagonet Ballads takes edge from the change in our circumstance. Ours, we are told, is an age fascinated by violence; but what of the morbid appeal of 'Sal Grogan's Face'?

> There on the right's Sal Grogan, leaning against the bar;
> Wait till she turns her head round—now you can see the scar.
> Isn't it something loathsome, that horribly weird grimace?—
> The burns that have blurred her features give her a demon's face.

The difference between us and the Victorians is less one of comparative violence than of clinical diagnosis. Sal Grogan's 'deed of grace' which ruined her beauty would be written off to-day as the grievous effect of a masochistic relationship. (But how much truer would that diagnosis be?)

The Matron's Story begins even more melodramatically.

> She was drunk—mad drunk—was Molly, the night I saw her first;
> I'd seen some terrible cases, but hers was the very worst.

Sims had the ability to engage attention from the very start. The ballads were splendid recitation pieces in the grand Victorian manner, slam bang and into top gear by the end of the first verse. But before we write off the melodrama of Sims's Ballads as ridiculous exaggeration, we should consider how much more exaggerated the public behaviour of the Victorians was in all matters except sex than our behaviour is to-day. Hymn books were brass bound in those days and rightly aimed could cut a cheek open: and fervent priests broke into brothels and gin-palaces flourishing crucifixes and asking 'Are you saved?' Often they made an impact on drunken audiences by their sheer audacity, but at other times they called down on themselves the fury from which Molly rescued 'our faithful priest'.

The stuff from which Sims made his ballads was of everyday life as he had witnessed it in his reporting. His dishonesty came in his arrangement of it. 'Billy's Rose' should be compared with his reportage on the Board Schools. Nell has been to Sunday school and been given a glimpse of religion. It was not inconceivable that Nell's vision of Heaven might be 'of a kind-eyed Saviour's love'.

> How He'd built for little children great big playgrounds up above,
> Where they sang and played at hop-scotch and at horses all the day,
> And where beadles and policemen never frightened them away.

But the setting in which the dying boy is left to be nursed by his eight-year-old sister, while her drunken parents are out on the booze is too simplified. There are in this slum no neighbours to keep an eye on the children; and little Nell is so dimwitted that she can't tell the difference between winter and summer. She runs all night out to the country. No rose, until a disdainful lady flings one from her 'chariot' in pique and Nelly picks it up and expires to take it to Billy in heaven.

Then Sims reached a nadir of mawkishness, deeper than Dickens ever plumbed with his little Nell or other child victims whose wrongs were redressed in Heaven. Sentimentality had never sunk lower; it belonged with the decadence of the Valentine, which had lost its earlier elegance among myriads of tinsel embellishments.

Yet besides its bathetic comedy, 'Billy's Rose' has a sociological interest. As well as, and perhaps more importantly than, being a reformer, George R. Sims was the assuager of the Victorian conscience.

As I have said, he pleaded for a wide variety of social measures. But he was realist enough to know that in his time the provision for the respectable poor would engage all the resources society could command. Education would teach the young better ways of life. Segregated housing would keep them from the contamination of the criminal classes. He absolved his generation of the sins of their fathers, provided that they did better by the rising generation.

But there still remained as a threat to complacence the high rate of child mortality. It was all very well to say that children who had been to Board School would grow up better than their parents. But what if they died of neglect before they left Board School? 'Billy's Rose' was an answer, a very inadequate answer, which was eagerly seized on by people as worried as Sims himself.

'The Road to Heaven' is a variation on the same theme as 'Billy's Rose.' The role of Nell is played by Jack 'a Sunday scholar' whose vision of heaven was 'a land of glory where the children sing all day'. Compared to his crippled companion Mike, Jack is lucky. Both his parents are dead and only his grandmother drinks his earnings from street-singing, whereas Mike has to support two drunken parents with his begging. Seeking Heaven in the Thames, Mike wakes up in hospital to ask the kind old doctor 'Please, are you God?' before passing away.

> This is the day of scoffers, but who shall say that night,
> When Mike asked the road to Heaven, that Jack didn't tell him right?
> 'Twas the children's Jesus pointed the way to the kingdom come
> For the poor little tired arab, the waif of a London slum.

Sims, no doubt, intended an irony, that Mike would be better dead that he could ever hope to be alive. But those who wished reassurance could believe that the cripple boy was compensated by eternal bliss.

I have tried to imagine the atmosphere in which Sims created his ballads. Was, for example, the germ of 'The Road to Heaven' a slum child in hospital asking the doctor, 'Please are you God?' I can believe this, since my elder daughter the first time she went to church, at the age of seven asked me the same question about the Vicar as he mounted the pulpit. But, supposing this was the germ of the poem, how did it grow?

Sims says that after he had finished his 'Mustard and Cress' column on a Friday evening, he would write a ballad at a single sitting, post it at 3 am and then go into the office and correct the proof in the

afternoon. The ballads were tossed off in a frenzy of histrionic impro-
visation. The mood was not one that could be sustained. It smells too
much of midnight oil. This was not daylight verse, composed in
Regent's Park watching the ducks. It was strong stuff, seventy per
cent proof.

Despite the assurances of Miss Minty Lamb, I believe that Sims
wrote the ballads after he had been drinking and probably imbibed
inspiration during their composition. Certainly no more dramatic
ballads were composed after Sims developed liver trouble and took
to lemon juice. He continued to write verse, but it was always of the
type called 'occasional', a quatrain in homage to de Hems, a poetic
testimonial to the Rendezvous Restaurant. The ballads could be
written easily under alcohol. The prosody was simple and emphatic;
the words were colloquial. What was creative was the construction,
an artificial neatness akin to the patterns of his dramas and short
stories. 'The Matron's Story', vastly improbable though it is, is magni-
ficently worked out, remote from reality, but as consistent within
itself as an exercise in non-Euclidian geometry. As literature, it may
be meretricious; but it has like all good bad verse the virtue of sin-
cerity. 'Billy's Rose' was intensely, if falsely, felt at the time. Sims
wrote his Ballads as fast as he wrote articles, always to the top of his
bent. Some were better than others, but none were written tongue
in cheek.

On the other hand, Sims rather enjoyed fun being made of his work.
He was amused when his friend and collaborator Henry Pettitt in a
Drury Lane drama gave one of the characters a compulsion to recite
'The Lifeboat'. Each time he announced 'I will now recite "The
Lifeboat",' he was silenced with 'The Lifeboat be hanged!' But Sims
was flattered when 'the gentleman who wished "The Lifeboat" that
fate had his wish gratified. "The Lifeboat" *was* hanged, or, rather,
hung. A well-known painter selected it as the subject of his Academy,
and it was hung—on the line.'

In the United States a flutter was caused by the ballad 'Ostler Joe',
which he had written for the actor Edmund Yates. It was a Drury
Lane melodrama *in petto*; the winsome wife of an ostler is seduced by
a wanton gentleman, becomes a theatrical cocotte and then as years
later she lies dying in poverty is sought out by her faithful husband.

In 1886, a Mrs Brown-Potter, a wealthy Washington socialite
ambitious of a theatrical career gave an amateur entertainment at the
house of Mrs Whitney. The *New York Times* reported:

Her reading of Swinburne's 'Hostler Joe' raised universal condemnation about the town and distressed and deeply embarrassed every man and woman in the chosen audience that had to listen to those indecent verses. As an attempted defence it is said that Mrs Potter first read the poem to three prominent society men, and they thought it very 'chic' and quite the thing. Again, it is claimed that only the title was named to the most prominent of the trio, and he, mistaking it for one of John Hay's dialect poems, thought that it would make a variety in the usual placid routine of amateur readings, and said, 'Read it.'

The embarrassed audience and the silence that reigned at the conclusion of the recitation were a sufficient intimation of the storm of censure that has since followed. As an instance of the depravity of the times it may be told that since that unfortunate night the libraries and book-stores have been besieged by people anxious to read the verses again, and the few known to own private copies of Swinburne's are overrun with borrowers.

The ascription of the poem to Swinburne was due presumably to the alliterative lushness of verses like

Yet a blossom I fain would pluck to-day from the garden above
    her dust;
Not the languorous lily of soulless sin nor the bloodred rose of
    lust;
But a sweet white blossom of holy love that grew in the one
    green spot
In the arid desert of Phryne's life, where all was parched and hot.

Having thumbed through the works of Swinburne in vain, some newspapermen announced that the author was not Algernon Charles Swinburne but William Gilmore Simms, author of *The Wigwam and the Cabin*. There followed a rush on the poems of W. G. Simms. It was not till this proved unproductive that the *New York World* printed the poem and ascribed it to 'the author of "The Lights o' London" '. The poem was copied elsewhere and various editions of *The Dagonet Ballads* were published. 'Ostler Joe' was read by about four fifths of the adult population of the United States. 'Mrs James Brown-Potter has done a wonderful thing for Mr George R. Sims,' said the *Chicago Daily Tribune*. 'His poem, "Ostler Joe"—and it is a pretty good poem—is being printed all over the country.'

According to one American newspaper, 667 leading articles were written on 'Ostler Joe' consisting of 4320 paragraphs, and 1285 news-papers reprinted the piece in full. It was recited in 290 theatres and referred to in 82 sermons. One publisher admitted that he had made $2,000 dollars out of the ballads in a fortnight.

A New York playwright wrote a play on 'Ostler Joe'. F. Belasco set the ballad to music for Tony Hart and in one of the *Mikado* companies Katisha recited it in a Japanese setting.

The rivalry to exploit 'Ostler Joe' grew sharper. At Koster and Bial's, James Gough made its recitation a star turn. Lilian Lewis, a Chicago actress who styled herself 'America's Own Dramatic Queen' claimed that George R. Sims had written 'Ostler Joe' specially for her. This was hotly denied by her fellow Chicagoan Anna Morgan, who claimed that she was the real and original reciter of the poem and all others, including Mrs Brown-Potter, were inferior imitators. The controversy became so sharp that the *New York Dramatic Mirror* proposed that a matinée should be devoted to a competitive reading by all claimants.

Interest in the poem became so acute that some American news-paper editors told their London correspondents to report on its author. 'I don't suppose Mr George R. Sims will be particularly satisfied when he learns of the tempest in a teapot his verses have created,' wrote one. 'He is rather a disagreeable man personally with a wonderful opinion of himself and an abominable temper. He has been singularly success-ful during the past five or six years, and I presume he has put aside enough money to make him independent for life.'

The genial Sims had good reason to be disagreeable. From U.S. newspaper, book, dramatic and performing rights, he did not receive a red cent.

*Exactly how much Sims earned a year, I don't know. But there is an interesting entry in Arnold Bennett's Journal for November 9, 1898.

'What do you suppose George R. Sims's income is?' Webster asked me. Webster is in the Income Tax department at Somerset House.

'Certainly over £15,000,' I said.

'Just what I think. Well, his assessment has recently been raised from £3,000 to £5,000, and he is kicking up an awful row about it. He comes up to the office himself several times a week, and argues and swears he will not pay.' *The Journals of Arnold Bennett*, Cassell, Vol. i. pp. 81/2.

In the last twenty years of his life, Sims was less vocal about the oppression of the poor than about the crippling of the middle class by taxation. The cost of the social reforms he had advocated was making itself felt. When he died, he left an estate of under £8,000, the result partly of his princely mode of living and partly of the gener-osity he shewed friends, acquaintances and even strangers in distress.

*Readings in Prose and Verse with Supplementary Lecture book, containing lectures and readings for the Magic Lantern, (price 1s) p. 205.

In England 'Ostler Joe' had already had a modest success. Madge Kendal had recited it at a fashionable charity matinée at a West End theatre without provoking the scandal which Mrs Brown-Potter had caused in Washington. In her memoirs Madge Kendal inferred that the poem had been written specially for *her*; and she certainly did her best to make it her own. She recited it at the Drury Lane for the American send-off of Lionel Brough and later at the St James's Hall introduced it into a concert given by Albani, Scalchi, Lloyd and Santley. 'There was not,' reported the *Lady*,' a dry eye in the room.'

In an age of tear-jerking, the Ballads of George R. Sims stood high; and it was natural that magic lantern slide makers should cash in, as far as possible without infringing copyright, as witness:

Nellie's Prayer
(Copyright)

The full reading of Nellie's Prayer is contained in the poem written by G. R. Sims Esq, which as this is copyright, we are not allowed to publish separately; it is published in a book with several other poems by the same author, and the price of it is 1s or 1s 3d post free. We are only able therefore, in this reading, to give a brief resumé of the various incidents to which the pictures refer.

The headings of the 12 slides are:

1. Called to the War.
2. He Kissed his darling Nellie.
3. She always prayed for Father.
4. Why are you crying Mammy?
5. A woman stooped and kissed her.
6. I fell on my knees and prayed.
7. I sat by the fireside, heartbroken.
8. Nellie was praying to God for her dear Dadda, not knowing that he was dead.
9. An angel watching over her.
10. Mammy, will father come home soon?
11. There was a quick step and the door opened.
12. Thank God for his blessed mercy, and His answer to Nellie's prayer.*

It can have been no easy task for the reciter to use these magic lantern-slides, even if he had known the name and address of the publisher of *The Lifeboat & other poems* in which 'Nellie's Prayer' appeared. Though it is possible to identify places for the first four slides, Nos 5 and 6 should be Nos 1 and 2, Nos 7 and 9 have nothing to do with the poem and the others only a vague connection. One suspects that the maker of the slides had not been able to afford a shilling or one and threepence post free.

But that the Ballads were rendered to magic lantern slides with powerful effect I am assured by Helen MacGregor who 'heard "Billy's Rose" recited by a perfervid teetotaler (I can, even after more than forty years, remember her formidable name, Mrs Murray MacIntyre) as an obligato to coloured magic lantern slides. In one of them, the children were playing "Hopscotch in Heaven!"'

Sims himself never refers to the use of magic lantern slides. Apart from the fact that he derived no royalty on their sale, he would probably have not approved of any distraction from the histrionics of the reciter. Slides took the attention from the performer, charming as they are in themselves. The ballads depended for their full effect on professional actors ready to wring the tear-ducts dry.

It was one of Dagonet's tribulations that he had to listen to amateur renderings. Just before the 1890 Derby, he went down to see the trial of the favourite Surefoot at Seven Barrows. That evening he was invited to meet the stable lads.

> I went, and it was with mixed feelings that I heard the vicar say, 'That lad is a fine reciter. You ought to hear him do your "Billy's Rose."'
>
> The stable lad, a smart young fellow, took the hint, stepped forward, and gave vent to the whole of the poem for my special benefit.
>
> Of course I shook him warmly by the hand and congratulated him, and I was right in doing so, for I observed as I turned away that he had brought tears to the eyes of several of the lads.

Tears did not come to the eyes of G. R. Sims until Surefoot starting at 95 to 40 on was beaten by Sainfoin.

In making this selection of ballads, I have omitted all Sims's Miscellaneous verse. Of the thirty seven narrative ballads, I have chosen what seem to-day most typical and topical. 'In the Shipka Pass' does not stir us as it would have stirred readers during the Russo–Turkish war of 1877–8; nor does the dying Communist of 'In a Cellar in Soho' do more than bewilder us when he implores just one boon ere he dies.

PREPARE TO SHED THEM NOW

When my soul clasps my own Marguerite,
And my body man lays to its rest,
Put her name on the stone at my feet
And a clod of French earth on my breast.

If much of what Sims wrote to provoke tears, inspires laughter, this is a tribute to reformers like Sims himself for making such poverty and suffering so unbelievable as to be ludicrous.

THE BALLADS

The slides which embellish the text of this edition were made in the 1890s by Bamforths of Holmfirth, using the factory staff as models against backcloths painted by Mr Bamforth at lightning speed.

BILLY'S ROSE

BILLY'S dead, and gone to glory—so is Billy's sister Nell:
There's a tale I know about them were I poet I would tell;
Soft it comes, with perfume laden, like a breath of country air
Wafted down the filthy alley, bringing fragrant odours there.

In that vile and filthy alley, long ago one winter's day,
Dying quick of want and fever, hapless, patient Billy lay,
While beside him sat his sister, in the garret's dismal gloom,
Cheering with her gentle presence Billy's pathway to the tomb.

PREPARE TO SHED THEM NOW

Many a tale of elf and fairy did she tell the dying child,
Till his eyes lost half their anguish, and his worn, wan features
    smiled:
Tales herself had heard hap-hazard, caught amid the Babel roar,
Lisped about by tiny gossips playing round their mothers' door.

Then she felt his wasted fingers tighten feebly as she told
How beyond this dismal alley lay a land of shining gold,
Where, when all the pain was over—where, when all the tears were
    shed—
He would be a white-frocked angel, with a gold thing on his head.

Then she told some garbled story of a kind-eyed Saviour's love,
How He'd built for little children great big playgrounds up above,
Where they sang and played at hop-scotch and at horses all the day,
And where beadles and policemen never frightened them away.

This was Nell's idea of Heaven—just a bit of what she'd heard,
With a little bit invented, and a little bit inferred.
But her brother lay and listened, and he seemed to understand,
For he closed his eyes and murmured he could see the Promised Land.

'Yes,' he whispered, 'I can see it—I can see it, sister Nell;
Oh, the children look so happy, and they're all so strong and well;
I can see them there with Jesus—He is playing with them, too!
Let us run away and join them if there's room for me and you.'

She was eight, this little maiden, and her life had all been spent
In the garret and the alley, where they starved to pay the rent;
Where a drunken father's curses and a drunken mother's blows
Drove her forth into the gutter from the day's dawn to its close.

But she knew enough, this outcast, just to tell the sinking boy,
'You must die before you're able all these blessings to enjoy.
You must die,' she whispered, 'Billy, and I am not even ill;
But I'll come to you, dear brother,—yes, I promise that I will.'

'You are dying, little brother,—you are dying, oh, so fast;
I heard father say to mother that he knew you couldn't last.
They will put you in a coffin, then you'll wake and be up there,
While I'm left alone to suffer in this garret bleak and bare.'

'Yes, I know it,' answered Billy. 'Ah, but, sister, I don't mind,
Gentle Jesus will not beat me; He's not cruel or unkind.
But I can't help thinking, Nelly, I should like to take away
Something, sister, that you gave me, I might look at every day.

'In the summer you remember how the mission took us out
To a great green lovely meadow, where we played and ran about,
And the van that took us halted by a sweet bright patch of land,
Where the fine red blossoms grew, dear, half as big as mother's hand.

'Nell, I asked the good kind teacher what they called such flowers as
    those,
And he told me, I remember, that the pretty name was rose.
I had never seen them since, dear—how I wish that I had one!
Just to keep and think of you, Nell, when I'm up beyond the sun.'

Not a word said little Nelly; but at night, when Billy slept,
On she flung her scanty garments and then down the stairs she crept.
Through the silent streets of London she ran nimbly as a fawn,
Running on and running ever till the night had changed to dawn.

When the foggy sun had risen, and the mist had cleared away,
All around her, wrapped in snowdrift, there the open country lay.
She was tired, her limbs were frozen, and the roads had cut her feet,
But there came no flowery gardens her poor tearful eyes to greet.

She had traced the road by asking—she had learnt the way to go;
She had found the famous meadow—it was wrapped in cruel snow;
Not a buttercup or daisy, not a single verdant blade
Showed its head above its prison. Then she knelt her down and
    prayed.

With her eyes upcast to heaven, down she sank upon the ground,
And she prayed to God to tell her where the roses might be found.
Then the cold blast numbed her senses, and her sight grew strangely
    dim;
And a sudden, awful tremor seemed to seize her every limb.

'Oh, a rose!' she moaned, 'good Jesus—just a rose to take to Bill!'
And as she prayed a chariot came thundering down the hill;
And a lady sat there, toying with a red rose, rare and sweet;
As she passed she flung it from her, and it fell at Nelly's feet.

Just a word her lord had spoken caused her ladyship to fret,
And the rose had been his present, so she flung it in a pet;
But the poor, half-blinded Nelly thought it fallen from the skies,
And she murmured, 'Thank you, Jesus!' as she clasped the dainty
    prize.

*   *   *   *

Lo that night from out the alley did a child's soul pass away,
From dirt and sin and misery to where God's children play.
Lo that night a wild, fierce snowstorm burst in fury o'er the land,
And at morn they found Nell frozen, with the red rose in her hand.

Billy's dead, and gone to glory—so is Billy's sister Nell;
Am I bold to say this happened in the land where angels dwell:—
That the children met in heaven, after all their earthly woes,
And that Nelly kissed her brother, and said, 'Billy, here's your rose'?

IN THE HARBOUR

o for a sail this mornin'?—This way, yer honour, please.
Weather about? Lor' bless you, only a pleasant breeze.
My boat's that there in the harbour, and the man aboard's
   my mate.
Jump in, and I'll row you out, sir; that's her, the Crazy Kate.

Queer name for a boat, you fancy; well, so it is, maybe,
But Crazy Kate and her story's the talk o' the place, you see;
And me and my pardner knowed her—knowed her all her life—
We was both on us asked to the weddin' when she was made a wife.

56

IN THE HARBOUR

Her as our boat's named arter was famous far and wide;
For years in all winds and weathers she haunted the harbour side,
With her great wild eyes a-starin' and a-strainin' across the waves,
Waitin' for what can't happen till the dead come out o' their graves.

She was married to young Ned Garling, a big brown fisher-lad;
One week a bride, and the next one a sailor's widow—and mad.
They were married one fearful winter, as widowed many a wife.
He'd a smile for all the lasses; but she loved him all her life.

A rollickin' gay young fellow, we thought her too good for him.
He'd been a bit wild and careless—but, married all taut and trim,
We thought as he'd mend his manners when he won the village prize,
And carried her off in triumph before many a rival's eyes.

But one week wed and they parted—he went with the fisher fleet—
With the men who must brave the tempest that the women and bairns
    may eat.
It's a rough long life o' partin's is the life o' the fisher folk,
And there's never a winter passes but some good-wife's heart is broke.

We've a sayin' among us sea folk as few on us dies in bed—
Walk through our little churchyard and read the tale of our dead—
It's mostly the bairns and the women as is restin' under the turf,
For half o' the men sleep yonder under the rollin' surf.

The night Kate lost her husband was the night o' the fearful gale—
She'd stood on the shore that mornin' and had watched the tiny sail
As it faded away in the distance—bound for the coast o' France,
And the fierce wind bore it swiftly away from her anxious glance.

The boats that had sailed that mornin' with the fleet were half a score,
And never a soul among 'em came back to the English shore.
There was wringin' o' hands and moanin', and when they spoke o'
   the dead
For many a long day after the women's eyes were red.

Kate heard it as soon as any—the fate of her fisherlad—
But her eyes were wild and tearless; she went slowly and surely mad.
'He isn't drowned,' she would murmur; 'he will come again some
   day'—
And her lips shaped the self-same story as the long years crept away.

Spring, and summer, and autumn—in the fiercest winter gale,
Would Crazy Kate stand watchin' for the glint of a far-off sail;
Stand by the hour together and murmur her husband's name—
For twenty years she watched there, for the boat that never came.

She counted the years as nothin'—the shock that had sent her mad
Had left her love for ever a brave, young, handsome lad;
She thought one day she should see him, just as he said good-bye,
When he leapt in his boat and vanished where the waters touched
   the sky.

She was but a lass when it happened—the last time I saw her there
The first faint streaks o' silver had come in her jetblack hair;
And then a miracle happened—her mad, weird words came right,
For the fisher lad came ashore, sir, one wild and stormy night.

We were all of us watchin', waitin', for at dusk we'd heard a cry,
A far-off cry, round the headland, and strained was every eye—
Strained through the deep'nin' darkness, and a boat was ready to
   man—
When, all of a sudden, a woman down to the surf-line ran.

PREPARE TO SHED THEM NOW

'Twas Crazy Kate. In a moment, before what she meant was known,
The boat was out in the tempest—and she was in it alone.
She was out of sight in a second—but over the sea came a sound,
The voice of a woman cryin' that her long-lost love was found.

A miracle, sir, for the woman came back through the ragin' storm,
And there in the boat beside her was lyin' a lifeless form.
She leapt to the beach and staggered, cryin', 'Speak to me, husband,
    Ned!'
As the light of our lifted lanterns flashed on the face o' the dead.

It was him as had sailed away, sir—a miracle sure it seemed.
We looked at the lad and knowed him, and fancied we must ha'
    dreamed—
It was twenty years since we'd seen him—since Kate, poor soul, went
    mad,
But there in the boat that evenin' lay the same brown handsome lad.

Gently we took her from him—for she moaned that he was dead—
We carried him to a cottage and we laid him on a bed;
But Kate came pushin' her way through and she clasped the lifeless
    clay,
And we hadn't the heart to hurt her, so we couldn't tear her away.

The news of the miracle travelled, and folks came far and near.
And the women talked of spectres—it had given 'em quite a skeer;
And the parson he came with the doctor down to the cottage quick—
They thought as us sea-folks' fancy had played our eyes a trick.

But the parson, who'd known Kate's husband, as had married 'em in
    the church,
When he seed the dead lad's features he gave quite a sudden lurch,
And his face was as white as linen—for a moment it struck him
    dumb—
I half expected he'd tell us as the Judgment Day was come.

60

IN THE HARBOUR

The Judgment Day, when the ocean they say 'ull give up its dead;
What else meant those unchanged features, though twenty years had
    sped?

          *   *   *   *

That night, with her arms around him, the poor mad woman died,
And here in our village churchyard we buried 'em side by side.

'Twas the shock, they said, as killed her—the shock o' seein' him
    dead.
The story got in the papers, and far and near it spread;
And some only half believed it—I know what you'd say, sir; wait—
Wait till you hear the finish o' this story o' Crazy Kate.

It was all explained one mornin' as clear as the light o' day,
And when we knowed we were happy to think as she'd passed
    away,
As she died with her arms around him, her lips on the lips o' the
    dead—
Believin' the face she looked on was the face o' the man she'd wed.

But the man she'd wed was a villain, and that she never knew—
He hadn't been drowned in the tempest; he only of all the crew
Was saved by a French ship cruising, and carried ashore, and there
Was nursed to life by a woman—a French girl, young and fair.

He fell in love with the woman—this dare-devil heartless Ned,
And married her, thinkin' the other had given him up for dead.
He was never the man—and we'd said so—for a lovin' lass like Kate;
But he mightn't ha' done what he did, sir, if he'd known of her cruel
    fate.

'Twas his son by the foreign woman, his image in build and face
Whose lugger the storm had driven to his father's native place—
'Twas his son who had come like a phantom out of the long ago.
On the spot where Kate had suffered God's hand struck Ned the blow.

We learnt it all from the parson when Ned came over the waves
In search o' the son he worshipped—and he found two fresh-made
   graves.
Dang!—what was that? Sit steady! Rowed right into you, mate!
I forgot where I was for a moment—I was tellin' the gent about Kate.

IN THE WORKHOUSE

CHRISTMAS DAY

IT is Christmas Day in the Workhouse,
    And the cold bare walls are bright
With garlands of green and holly,
    And the place is a pleasant sight:
For with clean-washed hands and faces,
    In a long and hungry line
The paupers sit at the tables,
    For this is the hour they dine.

And the guardians and their ladies,
  Although the wind is east,
Have come in their furs and wrappers,
  To watch their charges feast;
To smile and be condescending,
  Put pudding on pauper plates,
To be hosts at the workhouse banquet
  They've paid for—with the rates.

Oh, the paupers are meek and lowly
  With their 'Thank'ee kindly, mum's';
So long as they fill their stomachs,
  What matter it whence it comes?
But one of the old men mutters,
  And pushes his plate aside:
'Great God!' he cries; 'but it chokes me!
  For this is the day *she* died.'

The guardians gazed in horror,
  The master's face went white;
'Did a pauper refuse their pudding?'
  'Could their ears believe aright?'
Then the ladies clutched their husbands,
  Thinking the man would die,
Struck by a bolt, or something,
  By the outraged One on high.

But the pauper sat for a moment,
  Then rose 'mid a silence grim,
For the others had ceased to chatter,
  And trembled in every limb.
He looked at the guardians' ladies,
  Then, eyeing their lords, he said,
'I eat not the food of villains
  Whose hands are foul and red:

'Whose victims cry for vengeance
  From their dank, unhallowed graves.'
'He's drunk!' said the workhouse master.
  'Or else he's mad, and raves.'
'Not drunk or mad,' cried the pauper,
  'But only a hunted beast,
Who, torn by the hounds and mangled,
  Declines the vulture's feast.

'I care not a curse for the guardians,
  And I won't be dragged away.
Just let me have the fit out,
  It's only on Christmas Day
That the black past comes to goad me,
  And prey on my burning brain;
  I'll tell you the rest in a whisper,—
I swear I won't shout again.

'Keep your hands off me, curse you!
    Hear me right out to the end.
You come here to see how paupers
    The season of Christmas spend.
You come here to watch us feeding,
    As they watch the captured beast.
Hear why a penniless pauper
    Spits on your paltry feast.

'Do you think I will take your bounty,
    And let you smile and think
You're doing a noble action
    With the parish's meat and drink?
Where is my wife, you traitors—
    The poor old wife you slew?
Yes, by the God above us,
    My Nance was killed by you!

'Last winter my wife lay dying,
    Starved in a filthy den;
I had never been to the parish,—
    I came to the parish then.
I swallowed my pride in coming,
    For, ere the ruin came,
I held up my head as a trader,
    And I bore a spotless name.

'I came to the parish, craving
　　Bread for a starving wife,
Bread for the woman who'd loved me
　　Through fifty years of life;
And what do you think they told me,
　　Mocking my awful grief?
That "the House" was open to us,
　　But they wouldn't give "out relief."

I slunk to the filthy alley—
　　'Twas a cold, raw Christmas eve—
And the bakers' shops were open,
　　Tempting a man to thieve;
But I clenched my fists together,
　　Holding my head awry,
So I came to her empty-handed,
　　And mournfully told her why.

'Then I told her "the House" was open;
　　She had heard of the ways of *that*,
For her bloodless cheeks went crimson,
　　And up in her rags she sat,
Crying, "Bide the Christmas here, John,
　　We've never had one apart;
I think I can bear the hunger,—
　　The other would break my heart."

'All through that eve I watched her,
   Holding her hand in mine,
Praying the Lord, and weeping
   Till my lips were salt as brine.
I asked her once if she hungered,
   And as she answered "No,"
The moon shone in at the window
   Set in a wreath of snow.

'Then the room was bathed in glory,
   And I saw in my darling's eyes
The far-away look of wonder
   That comes when the spirit flies;
And her lips were parched and parted,
   And her reason came and went,
For she raved of our home in Devon,
   Where our happiest years were spent.

'And the accents, long forgotten,
   Came back to the tongue once more,
For she talked like the country lassie
   I woo'd by the Devon shore.
Then she rose to her feet and trembled,
   And fell on the rags and moaned,
And, "Give me a crust—I'm famished—
   For the love of God!" she groaned.

68

IN THE WORKHOUSE

'I rushed from the room like a madman,
　And flew to the workhouse gate,
Crying, "Food for a dying woman!"
　And the answer came, "Too late."
They drove me away with curses;
　Then I fought with a dog in the street,
And tore from the mongrel's clutches
　A crust he was trying to eat.

'Back, through the filthy by-lanes!
　Back, through the trampled slush!
Up to the crazy garret,
　Wrapped in an awful hush.
My heart sank down at the threshold,
　And I paused with a sudden thrill,
For there in the silv'ry moonlight
　My Nance lay, cold and still.

'Up to the blackened ceiling
　The sunken eyes were cast—
I knew on those lips all bloodless
　My name had been the last;
She'd called for her absent husband—
　O God! had I but known!—
Had called in vain, and in anguish
　Had died in that den—*alone*.

69

'Yes, there, in a land of plenty,
    Lay a loving woman dead,
Cruelly starved and murdered
    For a loaf of the parish bread.
At yonder gate, last Christmas,
    I craved for a human life.
You, who would feast us paupers,
    What of my murdered wife!

'There, get ye gone to your dinners;
    Don't mind me in the least;
Think of the happy paupers
    Eating your Christmas feast;
And when you recount their blessings
    In your smug parochial way,
Say what you did for *me,* too,
    Only last Christmas Day.'

NELLIE'S PRAYER

IT'S a month to-day since they brought me
    The news of my darling's death;
I knew what it meant when the neighbours
    Whispered under their breath;
And one good motherly creature,
    Seeing my Nell at play,
Stooped down, with her eyelids streaming,
    And kissed her and turned away.

71

I knew that my Nell was an orphan
    And I was a widowed wife,
That a soldier for Queen and country
    Had bravely given his life;
That out on the field of battle,
    Under the far-off skies,
He had thought of his absent dear ones
    With the film of death on his eyes.

It was there in the evening paper,
    His name was among the dead—
We had won a glorious battle,
    And the enemy, beaten, fled.
Then they counted the dead and wounded,
    And found him among the slain;
O God! had I known when we parted
    We were never to meet again!

I couldn't believe the story—
   I couldn't believe that he,
My darling—my soldier husband—
   Would never come back to me.
I had thought of him night and morning;
   I had passed long nights on my knees
Praying that God would bring him
   Back to me over the seas.

It all came back like a vision;
   I could hear the band as it played
When the regiment marched to the station,
   And the noise that the people made
As they shouted 'Good luck' to the soldiers.
   And gave them three ringing cheers,
While the women, with ashen faces,
   Walked by the side in tears.

We walked by *his* side that morning,
   And Nellie was quite elate
With the band and the crowd and the cheering—
   My Nellie was only eight.
She never thought of the danger;
   He had tried to make her gay,
And told her to take care of mother—
   He wouldn't be long away.

He held her up at the station,
   Lifted her up to kiss,
And then, with her arms flung round him,
   Said to her, softly, this:
'Nellie, my pet, at bed time,
   When you kneel at your mother's knee
To pray to the God who loves us,
   Say a wee prayer for me.

NELLIE'S PRAYER

'I shall think of you in the twilight,
    When the stars come out above,
And fancy I see you kneeling
    With your blue eye full of love,
Breathing my name to Heaven;
    And if, as the good folks say,
God hears the prayers of the children,
    He'll guard me while I'm away.

'He'll guard me, and bring me safely
    Back, little Nell, to you:
There's many a danger, darling,
    He'll have to help me through.'
And the child looked up at her father,
    The tears in her pretty eyes;
There was something of shame in her manner—
    Something of sad surprise.

'You needn't have asked me, daddy,
    I always do that!' she said;
'Don't I pray for you and for mammy
    At night when I go to bed?
God loves the little children,
    And answers their prayers, they say;
I'm sure that you'll come back safely,
    I'll ask in my prayers that you may.'

It's only a month since they started.
  We thought when the regiment went
That long ere the troops were landed
  The force of the war would be spent.
And so I had taken courage,
  And looked on the bright side first,
Though now and again I fretted,
  And sometimes feared the worst.

They took little Nellie from me,
  Took her away for a while;
How could I hear her prattle,
  And watch her eager smile,
As she counted the days till daddy
  Would be back from the foreign shore?
How could I tell my darling
  She would see his face no more?

I was left alone with my sorrow—
   Alone in my little room,
Where the evening shadows deepened
   Into the twilight gloom.
I had heard the words they uttered,
   I had seen his name on the list;
But I sat and peered through the darkness
   As a sailor peers through the mist.

I sat like a sleeper doubting
   If she dreams or is wide awake,
Till the truth came on me fiercely,
   And I thought that my heart would break.
As I sat in the deepening gloaming
   The child came back again,
And I picked her up and kissed her
   While my tears ran down like rain.

'Why are you crying, mammy?'
    I only shook my head.
'It's nothing, Nellie,' I whispered;
    'Kiss me, and go to bed.'
'Let me say my prayers, mammy—
    Will you hear me say them now?'
She prayed for her absent father;
    I listened, but God knows how.

She prayed to the Lord to bring him,
    Safe and sound and well,
Back from the far-off country
    To mother and little Nell—
Prayed *that*, with her father lying
    In that far-off country dead!
'Now, father's safe till ro-morrow,'
    She whispered, and went to bed.

I hadn't the heart to tell her,
  So night after night she prayed,
Just as she promised her father
  When the last good-bye he bade.
But the prayer was a cruel dagger
  To me as I sat and heard,
And my heart was stabbed to bleeding
  With every childish word.

So a weary month went over,
  Till at last my nerves gave way,
And I told her to stop one evening,
  As she came to my knee to pray.
My brain was turned with sorrow,
  I was wicked and weak and wild
To speak as I spoke that evening,
  And shock the faith of a child.

PREPARE TO SHED THEM NOW

She heard what I said; then, sobbing,
   Broke from my knee and fled
Up to her room, and I heard her
   Kneeling beside her bed.
She prayed in her childish fashion,
   But her words were choked with tears—
I had told her it wasn't always
   God the prayer of the children hears.

She prayed that her absent father
   Might come back safe and well,
From the perils of war and battle,
   To mother and little Nell.
And, ere ever her prayer was finished
   The door was opened wide,
And my darling rushed towards me—
   My darling who had died!

I gave one cry and I fainted,
   And Nell ran down at the cry:
'They said God wouldn't hear me,'
   She told him by-and-by.
When the shock of surprise was over
   We knew what the miracle meant,
There'd been a mistake in the bodies,
   And the news to the wrong wife sent.

There were two of his name in the regiment—
   The other was killed, and when
It came to making the list out
   An error was made in the men.
Yet I think as I clasp my darling,
   Would be still her here to-day
Had I shaken Nell's simple tenet,
   'God listens when children pray?'

SAL GROGAN'S FACE

THERE on the right's Sal Grogan, leaning against the bar;
    Wait till she turns her head round—now you can see the
      scar.
    Isn't it something loathsome, that horribly weird grimace?—
The burns that have blurred her features give her a demon's face.
She's worse than the wandering leper, for whenever she goes about
Folks shudder, and ask in anger, 'Who lets such monsters out?'
And yet if they knew her story, and how those wounds were got,
I fancy the hardest-hearted would pity her awful lot.

You wouldn't believe Sal Grogan, that poor, distorted wretch,
Was ever a fine young woman; and reckoned a decent catch,
Shapely and plump and pretty,—and many a good old pal,
Who lived in the court that she did, fell out for the love of Sal,—
Fell out and had fearful quarrels; and many and many a fight
There's been in this very gin-shop, for the hag you see to-night.
But Sally, she turned her nose up, and flouted the lot with pride.
Drink up your liquor, she hears us! I'll tell you the rest outside.

SAL GROGAN'S FACE

I couldn't have stood it much longer—that awful face of hers,
Those horrible wounds and wrinkles, that ghastly mass of blurs!
It's a sickening sight to look at—did you see how the features run?—
There, let me get on with my story,—Sal flouted 'em ev'ry one:
Then all of a sudden she married a fellow called Handsome Jack—
Went and got married one Sunday behind her father's back.
A decent chap was her father, as folks in alleys go,
And Sal had a very good reason for wishing him not to know.

Grogan had got the credit of being a bit too flash,
For nobody knew exactly how he got hold of cash;
He was always in bed in the day-time, and seldom went out till night,
And folks in the alley whispered, he *had* to keep out of sight.
But Sal she worshipped the fellow, never a doubt of that,
And if anyone spoke against him, she answered 'em plain and pat.
For a couple of years, or over, affairs went smooth and well,
Then suddenly down the alley gossips had tales to tell.

One had heard Grogan swearing, and had caught the sound of blows
(The walls were of lath-and-plaster, and the houses stood in rows);
Another had seen Sal crying, and noticed a bruise on her cheek,
And then the women remembered she'd stayed indoors for a week.
But at last the whole court knew it, for the sounds of the strife grew
   high,
And Sally ran out all bloody, with a big cut over her eye;
Jack at her heels came swearing, and straight at her throat he flew,
And beating her down he kicked her, splitting her cheek in two.

Then some of the women hissed him, but he gave her another kick
Right in the breast, and this time—Faugh! but it makes one sick
To tell of that deed inhuman—it's common enough, they say,
And down in these courts it happens pretty well every day.
Poor Sal was just like a dead thing, but they let Jack slink away,
And when he was safe, policemen were beckoned to where she lay.
They bundled her on to a stretcher, and carried her off to Guy's;
She was out in about a fortnight, with the loss of one of her eyes.

She yearned for her home and husband—for through all the weary
        time
He'd never been near to see her; she fancied he feared his crime.
She had sent him a gentle message, saying that she forgave;
She worshipped the man, remember; she was only his humble slave.
She came to her home, and entered, hoping to find him there;—
And she found him there, with another—a woman young and fair.
She knew the girl in a moment, 'twas a white-faced, simpering jade
She'd seen before with her husband when the seeds of strife were laid

She looked in his eyes a second, as she stood at the open door,
Then called on her God to witness he should see her face no more.
One glance of scorn and of loathing on the shameless pair she hurled,
Then gasping for breath she staggered out on the pitiless world.

*   *   *   *

Months slipped away, and Sal Grogan no more in the court was met
Till one night she was seen near her father's, talking to Hagan's Bet.
Her figure was shrunk and wasted, and her face had grown so thin
That the scum of the alley saw it, and hushed their infernal din.

SAL GROGAN'S FACE

But right on the sudden silence rang a woman's piercing cry,
As flames from the crowded houses shot roaring up in the sky.
It was but the work of a moment, the flames rose higher and higher,
And spread till the crazy buildings were wrapped in a sheet of fire.
The court was filled in an instant with the black and blinding smoke,
And the crowd surged down the entry—an easyish one to choke;
But high above all the uproar Sal heard a woman shout
That Jack was drunk in the building, and no one could get him out.

The white-faced wanton knew it—she'd left him there and fled;
'She'd tried to save him,' she snivelled, 'he was tipsy, asleep on
   the bed,
She couldn't help it—she tried to—but her life was her life, you
   know;
Let them as jawed so save him; why, it was death to go!'
The light o' love spoke truly, the flames had spread and spread;
Who went up that burning staircase might reckon themselves as dead.
Ha! what is that?—a woman?—by Heaven, the fellow's wife!
She has leapt in the fiery furnace! Sal Grogan! back for your life!

Too late—she has gone for ever—up to an awful death.
Men strain their eyes in terror, and the great crowd holds its breath.
'The roof is giving and melting!' As they shout the lead falls fast
In beads of the brightest silver, hot from the fiery blast.
Back went the crowd in a moment—it saw that the end was near—
And then with a rush ran forward, raising a deafening cheer:
For down through the falling timbers, down through the smoke and
   flame,
Bearing her heavy burden, the brave Sal Grogan came.

And just as she reached the bottom she staggered, and moaned, and
    fell,
But they dragged her, scorched and senseless, out of that burning hell.
She had paid a price for her daring, for full in her face, poor lass!
The molten lead had fallen and left it a scalded mass.
They thought that she'd die, but she didn't, for she lived to be the
    sight—
The horribly blemished creature you saw in the bar to-night.
She's taken to drink, they tell me. The husband? Oh, they say
He muttered a drunken 'Curse you!' and went off to his wench next
    day.

            *   *   *   *

Oh, who would shudder or sicken, if he knew of the deed of grace
Enshrined in the ghastly features of poor Sal Grogan's face!

OSTLER JOE

I STOOD at eve, as the sun went down, by a grave where a woman lies,
  Who lured men's souls to the shores of sin with the light of her wanton eyes,
Who sang the song that the Siren sang on the treacherous Lurley height,
Whose face was as fair as a summer day, and whose heart was as black as night.

Yet a blossom I fain would pluck to-day from the garden above her dust;
Not the languorous lily of soulless sin nor the bloodred rose of lust;
But a sweet white blossom of holy love that grew in the one green spot
In the arid desert of Phryne's life, where all was parched and hot.

87

PREPARE TO SHED THEM NOW

*　　　*　　　*　　　*

In the summer, when the meadows were aglow with blue and red,
Joe, the ostler of the Magpie, and fair Annie Smith were wed.
Plump was Annie, plump and pretty, with a cheek as white as snow;
He was anything but handsome was the Magpie's ostler, Joe.

But he won the winsome lassie. They'd a cottage and a cow,
And her matronhood sat lightly on the village beauty's brow.
Sped the months and came a baby—such a blue-eyed baby boy!
Joe was working in the stables when they told him of his joy.

He was rubbing down the horses, and he gave them then and there
All a special feed of clover, just in honour of the heir:
It had been his great ambition, and he told the horses so,
That the Fates would send a baby who might bear the name of Joe.

Little Joe the child was christened, and, like babies, grew apace;
He'd his mother's eyes of azure and his father's honest face.
Swift the happy years went over, years of blue and cloudless sky;
Love was lord of that small cottage, and the tempests passed them by.

Passed them by for years, when swiftly burst in fury o'er their home.
Down the lane by Annie's cottage chanced a gentleman to roam;
Thrice he came and saw her sitting by the window with her child,
And he nodded to the baby, and the baby laughed and smiled.

So at last it grew to know him—little Joe was nearly four;
He would call the 'pretty gemplun' as he passed the open door;
And one day he ran and caught him, and in child's play pulled him in,
And the baby Joe had prayed for brought about the mother's sin.

OSTLER JOE

'Twas the same old wretched story that for ages bards have sung:
'Twas a woman weak and wanton and a villain's tempting tongue;
'Twas a picture deftly painted for a silly creature's eyes
Of the Babylonian wonders and the joy that in them lies.

Annie listened and was tempted; she was tempted and she fell,
As the angels fell from heaven to the blackest depths of hell;
She was promised wealth and splendour and a life of guilty sloth,
Yellow gold for child and husband,—and the woman left them both.

Home one eve came Joe the Ostler with a cheery cry of 'Wife!'
Finding that which blurred for ever all the story of his life.
She had left a silly letter,—through the cruel scrawl he spelt;
Then he sought the lonely bed-room, joined his horny hands and
    knelt.

'Now, O Lord, O God, forgive her, for she ain't to blame!' he cried;
'For I owt t'a seen her trouble, and 'a gone away and died.
Why, a wench like her—God bless her!—'twasn't likely as her'd rest
With that bonny head for ever on a ostler's ragged vest.

'It was kind o' her to bear me all this long and happy time,
So for my sake please to bless her, though You count her deed a crime;
If so be I don't pray proper, Lord, forgive me; for You see
I can talk all right to 'osses, but I'm nervous like with Thee.'

Ne'er a line came to the cottage from the woman who had flown;
Joe the baby died that winter, and the man was left alone.
Ne'er a bitter word he uttered, but in silence kissed the rod,
Saving what he told his horses, saving what he told his God.

Far away in mighty London rose the woman into fame,
For her beauty won men's homage, and she prospered in her shame;
Quick from lord to lord she flitted, higher still each prize she won,
And her rivals paled beside her as the stars beside the sun.

Next she made the stage her market, and she dragged Art's temple
    down
To the level of a show place for the outcasts of the town.
And the kisses she had given to poor Ostler Joe for nought
With their gold and costly jewels rich and titled lovers bought.

Went the years with flying footsteps while her star was at its height;
Then the darkness came on swiftly, and the gloaming turned to night.
Shattered strength and faded beauty tore the laurels from her brow;
Of the thousands who had worshipped never one came near her now.

Broken down in health and fortune, men forgot her very name,
Till the news that she was dying woke the echoes of her fame;
And the papers in their gossip mentioned how an 'actress' lay
Sick to death in humble lodgings, growing weaker every day.

One there was who read the story in a far-off country place,
And that night the dying woman woke and looked upon his face.
Once again the strong arms clasped her that had clasped her long ago,
And the weary head lay pillowed on the breast of Ostler Joe.

All the past had he forgotten, all the sorrow and the shame;
He had found her sick and lonely, and his wife he now could claim.
Since the grand folks who had known her one and all had slunk away,
He could clasp his long-lost darling, and no man would say him nay.

In his arms death found her lying, in his arms her spirit fled;
And his tears came down in torrents as he knelt beside her dead.
Never once his love had faltered through her base unhallowed life;
And the stone above her ashes bears the honoured name of wife.

*   *   *   *

That's the blossom I fain would pluck to-day from the garden above
    her dust;
Not the languorous lily of soulless sin nor the blood-red rose of lust;
But a sweet white blossom of holy love that grew in the one green spot
In the arid desert of Phryne's life, where all was parched and hot.

TICKET-O'-LEAVE

A VILLAGE DRAMA

WHO'S getting married this morning? Some o' the big folks? No!
Leastways, not as you'd call such as nowadays big folks go.
It's only a common wedding—old Bradley's daughter Eve
Is a-saying 'I will' in yonder, and the bridegroom's 'Ticket-o'-Leave.'

You thought 'twas a big folk's wedding because o' the crowd, maybe;
Well, it's one as the whole o' the village has come to the church to see.
You needn't say you're a stranger—if you wasn't you'd know their tale,
For to find another as didn't you might search ten mile and fail.

'Ticket-o'-Leave,' did I call him? I did, sir, and all round here
'Ticket-o'-Leave' we've called him for as nigh as maybe a year;
For he came back here from a prison—this is his native place,
And that was the gibe as his neighbours flung in his haggard face.

Eve was the village beauty, with half the lads at her feet;
But she only gave 'em the chaff, sir—it was Ned as got all the wheat.
They were sweethearts trothed and plighted, for old Bradley was
   nothing loth—
He had kissed the girl when she told him, and promised to help them
   both.

But Jack, his son, was his idol—a rackety, scapegrace lad;
Though to speak e'er a word agin him was to drive the old chap mad.
He worshipped the boy—God help him!—the dearest to him on
   earth:
The wife of his early manhood had died in giving him birth.

To him Jack was just an angel; but over the village ale
The gossips who knew his capers could tell a different tale.
There were whispers of more than folly—of drinking bouts and of
   debt,
And of company Jack was keeping into which it was bad to get.

Ned heard it all at the alehouse, smoking his pipe one night,
And he struck his fist on the table, and gave it them left and right;
He said it was lies, and dared them to breathe a word 'gin the lad—
He feared it might reach the farmer; but Ned knew as the boy was
   bad.

Old Bradley was weak and ailing, the doctor had whispered Ned
That a sudden shock would kill him—that he held his life by a thread.
So that made Ned more than anxious to keep the slanders back
That were running rife in the village about the scapegrace Jack.

One night—I shall ne'er forget it, for it came like a thunderclap—
The news came into the village as they'd found a pedlar chap
Smothered in blood and senseless, shot and robbed on the green,
And they brought Ned back here handcuffed two constables between.

At first we couldn't believe it, not as he could ha' been the man,
But one of our chaps had caught him just as he turned and ran—
Had caught Ned there red-handed, with a gun and the pedlar's gold,
And we went in a crowd to the station, where the rest of the tale
    was told.

The facts agin Ned were damning. When they got the pedlar round
His wound was probed, and a bullet that fitted Ned's gun was found.
He'd been shot from behind a hedgerow, and had fallen and swooned
    away,
And Ned must have searched his victim and have robbed him as he
    lay.

They kept it back from the farmer, who had taken at last to his bed:
Eve came, red-eyed, and told him that she'd had a quarrel with Ned,
And he'd gone away and had left them, and p'r'aps he wouldn't come
   back—
Old Bradley said he was sorry, then asked for his boy, his Jack.

And Jack, white-faced and trembling, he crept to his father's side,
And was scarcely away from the homestead till after the old man died.
On the night that death crossed the threshold one last, long, lingering
   look
At the face that was his dead darling's the poor old farmer took.

As the shadows of twilight deepened the long ago came back,
And his weak voice faintly whispered, 'Lean over and kiss me, Jack;
Let me take your kiss to Heaven, to the mother who died for you.'
And Eve sobbed out as she heard him, 'Thank God, he never knew!'

In his lonely cell a felon heard of the old man's end
In a letter his faithful sweetheart had conquered her grief to send;
And the load of his pain was lightened as he thought of what might
    have been
Had Jack and not he been taken that night upon Parson's Green.

Five years went over the village, and then, one midsummer eve,
Came Ned back here as an outcast—out on his ticket-o'-leave;
And all of the people shunned him; the Bradleys had moved away,
For Jack had squandered the money in drink and in vice and play.

Poor Eve was up at the doctor's—his housekeeper, grave and staid;
There was something about her manner that made her old flames
    afraid.
Not one of them went a-wooing—they said that her heart was dead,
That it died on the day the judges sentenced her sweetheart Ned.

'Ticket-o'-Leave' they called him after he came back here:
God knows what he did for a living!—he must ha' been starved pretty
    near.
But he clung to the village somehow—got an odd job now and then;
But, whenever a farmer took him, there was grumbling among the
    men.

He was flouted like that for a twelvemonth. Then suddenly came a
    tale
That a man from out of our village had been sick in the county gaol—
Sick unto death, and, dying, he had eased his soul of a sin,
Hoping by that atonement some mercy above to win.

We knew it all on Sunday, for the parson, right out in church,
He wiped away in a moment from Ned the felon smirch.
He told us his noble story; how, following Jack that night,
He had seen him shoot at the pedlar, and rob him and take to flight.

He had seized the gun and the money from the rascal's trembling
   hand;
Jack fled at the sound of footsteps, and the rest you can understand.
The word that he might have spoken Ned kept to himself to save,
For the sake of the dying father, the pitiful thief and knave.

He knew that the blow would hasten the death of one who had done
More for him than a father—who had treated him as a son;
And so he suffered in silence, all through the weary years,
The felon's shame and the prison, and the merciless taunts and jeers.

Hark! there's the organ pealing. See how the crowd divides!
Room for the best of fellows!—room for the queen of brides!
Look at their happy faces! Three cheers for the faithful Eve!
And three times three and another for Ned, the 'Ticket-o'-Leave!'

TOLD TO THE MISSIONARY

UST look 'ee here Mr. Preacher, you're a-goin' a bit too fur;
There isn't the man as is livin' as I'd let say a word agen her
She's a rum-lookin' bitch, that I own to, and there *is* a fierce
look in her eyes,
But if any cove sez as she's vicious, I sez in his teeth, he lies.
Soh! gently, old 'ooman; come here, now, and set by my side on
the bed;
I wonder who'll have yer, my beauty, when him as you're all to's
dead!
There, stow your perlaver a minit; I knows as my end is nigh;
Is a cove to turn round on his dog, like, just 'cos he's goin' to die?

Oh, of course, I was sartin you'd say it. It's allus the same with you,
Give it us straight now, guv'nor,—what would you have me do?
Think of my soul? I do, sir. Think of my Saviour?—Right!
Don't be afeared of the bitch, sir; *she's* not a-goin' to bite.
Tell me about my Saviour—tell me that tale agen,
How He prayed for the coves as killed Him, and died for the worst
of men.
It's a tale as I always liked, sir; and bound for the 'ternal shore,
I thinks it aloud to myself, sir, and I likes it more and more.

TOLD TO THE MISSIONARY

I've thumbed it out in the Bible, and I know it now by heart,
And it's put like steam in my boiler, and made me ready to start.
I ain't not afeared to die now; I've been a bit bad in my day,
But I know when I knocks at them portals there's One as won't say
   me nay.
And it's thinkin' about that story, and all as He did for us,
As makes me so fond o' my dawg, sir, specially now I'm wus;
For a-savin' o' folks who'd kill us is a beautiful act, the which
I never heard tell on o' no one, 'cept o' Him and o' that there bitch.

Yes, you may open yer eyes, sir—but I say by the Lord it's true!
I ha' told the story often; sit 'e down, while I tell it to you.
Dang this 'ere coughin', it stops me—it's a cold I caught last year,
As has tumbled my ninepins over, and lef me a-dyin here.
I was out on the drunk and caught it—lor, what a cuss is drink!—
But there, when a cove's as I am, it don't do him good to think.
I must cut it yer short, I reckon, for whenever I tries to speak
I feels like a bloomin' babby—I gets so infernal weak.

'Twas five years ago come Chrismus, maybe you remember the row,
There was scares about hydryphoby—same as there be just now;
And the bobbies came down on us costers—came in a reggerlar wax,
And them as 'ud got no licence was summerned to pay the tax.
But I had a friend among 'em, and he come in a friendly way,
And he sez, 'You must settle your dawg, Bill, unless you've a mind
   to pay.'
The missus was dyin' wi' fever—I'd made a mistake in my pitch,
I *couldn't* afford to keep her, so I sez, 'I'll drownd the bitch!'

PREPARE TO SHED THEM NOW

I wasn't a-goin' to *lose* her, I warn't such a brute, you bet,
As to leave her to die by inches o' hunger, and cold and wet;
I never said now't to the missus—we both on us liked her well—
But I takes her the follerin' Sunday down to the Grand Canell.
I gets her tight by the collar—the Lord forgive my sin!
And, kneelin' down on the towpath, I ducks the poor beast in.
She gave just a sudden whine like, then a look come into her eyes
As 'ull last for ever in mine, sir, up to the day I dies.

And a chill came over my heart then, and thinkin' I heard her moan,
I held her below the water, beating her skull with a stone.
You can see the mark of it now, sir—that place on the top of 'er 'ed—
And sudden she ceased to struggle, and I fancied as she was dead.
I shall never know how it happened, but goin' to loose my hold,
My knees slipped over the towpath, and into the stream I rolled;
Down like a log I went, sir, and my eyes were filled with mud,
And the water was tinged above me with a murdered creeter's blood.

I gave myself up for lost then, and I cursed in my wild despair,
And sudden I rose to the surfis, and a su'thing grabbed my hair—
Grabbed at my hair, and loosed it, and grabbed me agin by the throat,
And *she* was a-holdin' my 'ed up, and somehow I kep' afloat.
I can't tell yer 'ow she done it, for I never know'd no more,
Till somebody seized my collar, and giv' me a lug ashore;
And my head was queer and dizzy, but I see as the bitch was weak,
And she lay on her side a-pantin', waitin' for me to speak.

What did I do with *her,* eh? You'd a hardly need to ax,
But I sold my barrer a Monday, an' paid the bloomin' tax.

         *   *   *   *

That's right, Mr. Preacher, pat her—you ain't not afeard on her now!—
Dang this here tellin' o' stories—look at the muck on my brow!

I'm weaker, an' weaker, an' weaker; I fancy the end ain't fur,
But you know why here on my deathbed I think o' the Lord and her.
And He who by men's hands tortured uttered that prayer divine,
'Ull pardon me linkin' Him like with a dawg as forgave like mine.
When the Lord in His mercy calls me to my last eternal pitch,
I know as you'll treat her kindly—promise to take my bitch!

THE STREET TUMBLERS

THANK the lady, Johnny, and give the money to dad;
Yes, I'm his mother, lady—don't say, 'Poor little lad!'
For he likes the tumblin' rarely—took to it from the first.
Accidents?—nothing to speak of—a bruise or two at the worst.
It's him as draws the money; he's pretty and looks so smart,
He gets many a bit o' silver, with a 'Bless your little heart!'
Danger—because his father flings him up like a ball?—
He's been at the game too long, ma'am, to let our Johnny fall.

THE STREET TUMBLERS

You'd sooner your child was dead, ma'am, than leading a life like
    this?
Come here a minute, Johnny, and give your mammy a kiss;
Look at his rosy cheeks, ma'am! look at his sturdy limbs!
Look how his dark eyes glisten! there's nothin' their brightness dims.
We live in the air and sunshine, we tramp thro' the long green lanes,
We know where to get good shelter, and we never have aches or pains.
We're happy we three together as we roam from place to place,
We should die pent up in cities, for we come of a gipsy race.

The rough and the smooth together, it isn't so hard a life.
Yes, I've had my troubles—the biggest, the year I was mother and
    wife.
'Twas a hard black frosty winter the year that our baby came,
The master had sprained his ankle, and hobbled along dead lame.
He'd had to give up performin', for the agony made him shriek,
And I had a month-old baby, and illness had left me weak.
We couldn't do much for a livin', and we weren't the folks to beg;
The master was fond o' baby, but, Lord, how he cursed his leg!

We wouldn't go in the workhouse, so we just kept trampin' on,
'Till the last of our little savin's hoarded for months had gone.
The master he got no better, and I got worse and worse,
And I watched the baby wastin' as I hadn't the strength to nurse.
I was cross and low, and I fretted, and I'd look at the child and think
As p'r'aps it 'ud be a mercy if the Lord 'ud let it sink—
Sink and die and be buried before it grew to know
What a road life is to travel when the luck's agin' your show.

PREPARE TO SHED THEM NOW

At last, with the miles of trampin', Jo's leg grew quite inflamed,
And the doctor who saw it told him if he didn't rest he'd be lamed;
You can fancy what that meant, lady, to him as could lie in the street
And toss a weight up and catch it, and spin it round with his feet.
Now we couldn't earn a copper, and at last we wanted bread,
So we had to go to the workhouse for the sake of a meal and bed.
We had to go to the workhouse, where they parted man and wife,
And that was the wretchedest time, ma'am, of all my wand'rin' life.

It's only folks like ourselves, ma'am, as can tell what artists feels,
When they're treated like common loafers that tramps and cadges and
 steals.
It seemed to us like a prison, with all them heartless rules,
So we started again, but often I'd stop by one o' them pools
That lie in a quiet corner, dark and slimy and still,
And wonder what drownin' felt like—you see I was weak and ill.
I know it was bad and sinful, but my thoughts were strange and wild;
You can pity a homeless mother, who loved her ailin' child.

I hated the healthy babies I saw in their mothers' arms,
I'd look at my pale thin darlin' with a thousand wild alarms,
And think of what lay before us if the master didn't mend,
And our means of earnin' a livin' had come to a sudden end.
I envied the sturdy children when I looked at my poor wee mite.
I sometimes fancy now, ma'am, maybe as my head weren't right;
But I never envied another after a certain day,
As Providence gave me a lesson in a wonderful sort o' way.

THE STREET TUMBLERS

It was through your a-sayin' you'd rather your child was stiff and
   dead
Than leadin' a life like Johnny, and as put it into my head
To tell you my bit o' story, and how as I came to see
It's better to be contented, no matter how bad things be.
Now look at him yonder, lady—handsome and firm o' limb;
There isn't a mother in England as mightn't be proud o' him.
Yet the day as I had my lesson I looked at his poor pinched face,
And I envied a little creature as came of a highborn race.

We'd tramped to a country village, and passin' the village church
Sat down in the porch a minute, for Joe had begun to lurch
And stagger a bit and murmur, for his ankle was awful bad;
But we hadn't sat down a second when a beadle came up like mad,
And ordered us off, and bellowed, and went nigh black in the face;
We saw what was up directly, when a big crowd filled the place,
And carriages full of ladies came drivin' up to the gate;
I never saw such a christenin'—'twas the heir to a grand estate.

We were pushed along by the people, and got mixed up in the crowd,
And I heard 'twas a countess's baby, for the women talked aloud.
The great folks filled the chancel—all friends of my lord the earl's,
For this was the first boy-baby—the others had all been girls.
I heard that one-half the county would come to that baby-boy;
I watched as his grand nurse held him, and I saw the mother's joy.
Then I thought of the life of pleasure, of the love and the tender care,
Of that fortune that God had given that white-robed baby-heir.

Then I looked at my half-starved Johnny, and thought of his hapless
   lot,
A lame street-tumbler's baby, by God and by man forgot.
And my heart was filled with passion as I looked at the tiny heir,
And thought, 'Ah, if only Johnny had future half as fair!'
I envied my lady countess—no fear had she for her child;
My eyes were red with weepin'—her proud lips only smiled,
And I cried in my bitter anguish, 'O God, if my little son
Could have such a fate as Heaven intends for that pampered one!'

So we stood in that church—two mothers—she blessed and me
   accursed,
And my heart was full of envy, when suddenly with a burst
Of a music loud and joyous the organ filled the place;
And stoopin', the lovely countess pressed her lips on her baby's face.
And then—it was all in a moment—I heard a sudden cry,
And a shriek from the lady-mother—then a murmur from low and
   high.
For the baby-heir to the title, guarded from every harm,
Lay dead in its christenin' garments—lay dead in its nurse's arm!

I rushed from the church that moment, my senses seemed to reel,
And I hugged my poor wee baby, with my hand on its heart to feel
The beatin' that seemed like music—then I clasped it to my breast
And smothered its face with kisses till I woke it from its rest.
Then its eyes looked up so sweetly, like an angel's, into mine,
And I thanked the God of Mercy for a blessing so divine.
For I had my babe—my darlin'—what matter the workhouse bed?
I could pity the noble lady, whose little child lay dead.

But our luck got round soon after, for I got better so quick
I was able to dance and juggle, and spin the hat with a stick;
And Johnny grew plump and pretty, and learnt to hold the shell,
To lisp out 'Ta' for the pennies, and the master's leg got well;
And then when the boy grew bigger he took to the tumblin' so
That he learnt the tricks directly, and was quite a part of the show.
Street tumblin' ain't a fortune, but you know how I came to see
As it's better to rest contented, to be what you've got to be.

THE LIFEBOAT

BEEN out in the lifeboat often? Ay, ay, sir, oft enough.
When it's rougher than this? Lor' bless you! this ain't what *we* calls rough!
It's when there's a gale a-blowin', and the waves run in and break
On the shore with a roar like thunder and the white cliffs seem to shake;
When the sea is a hell of waters, and the bravest holds his breath
As he hears the cry for the lifeboat—his summons maybe to death—
That's when we call it rough, sir; but, if we can get her afloat,
There's always enough brave fellows ready to man the boat.

THE LIFEBOAT

You've heard of the Royal Helen, the ship as was wrecked last year?
Yon be the rock she struck on—the boat as went out be here;
The night as she struck was reckoned the worst as ever we had,
And this is a coast in winter where the weather be awful bad.
The beach here was strewed with wreckage, and to tell you the truth,
   sir, then
Was the only time as ever we'd a bother to get the men.
The single chaps was willin', and six on 'em volunteered,
But most on us here is married, and the wives that night was skeered.

Our women ain't chicken-hearted when it comes to savin' lives,
But death that night looked certain—and our wives be only wives;
Their lot ain't bright at the best, sir; but here, when the man lies dead,
'Tain't only a husband missin', it's the children's daily bread;
So our women began to whimper and beg o' the chaps to stay—
I only heerd on it after, for that night I was kept away.
I was up at my cottage, yonder, where the wife lay nigh her end,
She'd been ailin' all the winter, and nothin' 'ud make her mend.

The doctor had given her up, sir, and I knelt by her side and prayed,
With my eyes as red as a babby's, that Death's hand might yet be
   stayed.
I heerd the wild wind howlin', and I looked on the wasted form,
And thought of the awful shipwreck as had come in the ragin' storm;
The wreck of my little homestead—the wreck of my dear old wife,
Who'd sailed with me forty years, sir, o'er the troublous waves of
   life,
And I looked at the eyes so sunken, as had been my harbour lights,
To tell of the sweet home haven in the wildest, darkest nights.

She knew she was sinkin' quickly—she knew as her end was nigh,
But she never spoke o' the troubles as I knew on her heart must lie,
For we'd had one great big sorrow with Jack, our only son—
He'd got into trouble in London, as lots o' the lads ha' done;
Then he'd bolted, his masters told us—he was allus what folk call wild.
From the day as I told his mother, her dear face never smiled.
We heerd no more about him, we never knew where he went,
And his mother pined and sickened for the message he never sent.

I had my work to think of; but she had her grief to nurse,
So it eat away at her heartstrings, and her health grew worse and
    worse.
And the night as the Royal Helen went down on yonder sands,
I sat and watched her dyin', holdin' her wasted hands.
She moved in her doze a little, then her eyes were opened wide,
And she seemed to be seekin' somethin', as she looked from side to
    side;
Then half to herself she whispered, 'Where's Jack, to say good-bye?
It's hard not to see my darlin', and kiss him afore I die!'

I was stoopin' to kiss and soothe her, while the tears ran down my
    cheek,
And my lips were shaped to whisper the words I couldn't speak,
When the door of the room burst open, and my mates were there
    outside
With the news that the boat was launchin'. 'You're wanted!' their
    leader cried.
'You've never refused to go, John; you'll put these cowards right.
There's a dozen of lives maybe, John, as lie in our hands to-night!'
'Twas old Ben Brown, the captain; he'd laughed at the women's
    doubt.
We'd always been first on the beach, sir, when the boat was goin' out.

THE LIFEBOAT

I didn't move, but I pointed to the white face on the bed—
'I can't go, mate,' I murmured; 'in an hour she may be dead.
I cannot go and leave her to die in the night alone.'
As I spoke Ben raised his lantern, and the light on my wife was thrown;
And I saw her eyes fixed strangely with a pleading look on me,
While a tremblin' finger pointed through the door to the ragin' sea.
Then she beckoned me near, and whispered, 'Go, and God's will be
   done!
For every lad on that ship, John, is some poor mother's son.'

Her head was full of the boy, sir—she was thinking, maybe, some
   day
For lack of a hand to help him his life might be cast away.
'Go, John, and the Lord watch o'er you! and spare me to see the light,
And bring you safe,' she whispered, 'out of the storm to-night.'
Then I turned and kissed her softly, and tried to hide my tears,
And my mates outside, when they saw me, set up three hearty cheers;
But I rubbed my eyes wi' my knuckles, and turned to old Ben and
   said,
'I'll see her again, maybe, lad, when the sea gives up its dead.'

We launched the boat in the tempest, though death was the goal in
   view,
And never a one but doubted if the craft could live it through;
But our boat she stood it bravely, and, weary and wet and weak,
We drew in hail of the vessel we had dared so much to seek.
But just as we come upon her she gave a fearful roll,
And went down in the seethin' whirlpool with every livin' soul!
We rowed for the spot, and shouted, for all around was dark—
But only the wild wind answered the cries from our plungin' bark.

I was strainin' my eyes and watchin', when I thought I heard a cry,
And I saw past our bows a somethin' on the crest of a wave dashed
    by;
I stretched out my hand to seize it. I dragged it aboard, and then
I stumbled, and struck my forrud, and fell like a log on Ben.
I remember a hum of voices, and then I knowed no more
Till I came to my senses here, sir—here, in my home ashore.
My forrud was tightly bandaged, and I lay on my little bed—
I'd slipped, so they told me arter, and a rulluck had struck my head.

Then my mates came in and whispered; they'd heard I was comin'
    round.
At first I could scarcely hear 'em, it seemed like a buzzin' sound;
But as soon as my head got clearer, and accustomed to hear 'em speak,
I knew as I'd lain like that, sir, for many a long, long week.
I guessed what the lads was hidin', for their poor old shipmate's sake.
I could see by their puzzled faces they'd got some news to break;
So I lifts my head from the pillow, and I says to old Ben, 'Look here!
I'm able to bear it now, lad—tell me, and never fear.'

Not one on 'em ever answered, but presently Ben goes out,
And the others slinks away like, and I says, "What's this about?
Why can't they tell me plainly as the poor old wife is dead?'
Then I fell again on the pillows, and I hid my achin' head;
I lay like that for a minute, till I heard a voice cry 'John!'
And I thought it must be a vision as my weak eyes gazed upon;
For there by the bedside, standin' up and well was my wife.
And who do ye think was with her? Why, Jack, as large as life.

THE LIFEBOAT

It was him as I'd saved from drownin' the night as the lifeboat went
To the wreck of the Royal Helen; 'twas that as the vision meant.
They'd brought us ashore together, he'd knelt by his mother's bed,
And the sudden joy had raised her like a miracle from the dead;
And mother and son together had nursed me back to life,
And my old eyes woke from darkness to look on my son and wife.
Jack? He's our right hand now, sir; 'twas Providence pulled him
    through—
He's allus the first aboard her when the lifeboat wants a crew.

TWO WOMEN

TO-NIGHT is a midnight meeting, and the Earl is in the chair;
There's food and a little sermon for all who enter there, ⸱⸱
For all of our erring sisters who, finding their trade is slack,
Have time to sit down and listen to the holy men in black.

To-night is a midnight meeting, and in from the filthy street
They are bringing the wretched wantons who sin for a crust to eat;
There's cake to be had, and coffee, as well as the brimstone tracts
That paint in such flaming colours the end of their evil acts.

There's cake to be had, and coffee, and a seat, and warmth and light,
And shelter, for just a little, from the pitiless lash of night;
And as for the scolding sermon—though it comes through the
    preacher's nose—
There's a bit of it, now and then, too, that tells on the ghastly rows.

TWO WOMEN

There are streaks on the ruddled faces when a long-lost chord is
   struck;
For women are quick to whimper when they're ill and are out of luck.
Some picture of early childhood—of the innocent long ago,
Is raised by an artful preacher, and the tears begin to flow.

It is only a trick of the platform, a trick that they always try,
For they reckon it half the battle if the women are made to cry;
They soften them down and smooth them, and then when they're
   ripe for seed,
They paint them an awful picture of the end of the life they lead.

To-night is a midnight meeting, and out of the rain and dirt
There creeps in a sinful woman—drenched is her draggled·skirt,
Drenched are the gaudy feathers that droop in her shapeless hat,
And her hair hangs over her shoulders in a wet, untidy mat.

She hears of the fiery furnace that waits for the wicked dead;
Of the torture in store for the outcast who sins for her daily bread;
She hears that a God of mercy has built, on a sunlit shore,
A haven of rest eternal for those who shall sin no more.

Anon by the silent waters she kneels, with her eyes upcast,
And whispers her Heavenly Father, 'O God, I have sinned my last.
Here, in this cruel city, to live I must sin the sin;
Save me from that, O Father!—pity, and take me in.'

A plunge in the muddy river, a cry on the chill night air,
And the waters upon their bosom a pilgrim sister bear;
She has laved the stain of the city from her soul in the river slime,
She has sought for the promised haven through the door of a deadly
   crime.

PREPARE TO SHED THEM NOW

*　　　*　　　*　　　*

To-night is a midnight meeting—a ball in a Western square—
And rank and fashion and beauty, and a Prince of the blood are there;
In the light of a thousand tapers the jewelled bosoms gleam,
And the cheeks of the men are flushing, and the eyes of the women
　beam.

Round in the sensuous galop the high-born maids are swung,
Clasped in the arms of *roués* whose vice is on ev'ry tongue;
And the stately Norman mothers look on the scene with pride
If the *roué* is only wealthy and in search of a youthful bride.

But fair above all the women is the beautiful Countess May,
And wealthy and great and titled yield to her queenly sway;
Her they delight to honour, her they are proud to know,
For wherever the Countess visits, a Prince of the blood will go.

The story is common gossip; there isn't a noble dame
That bows to the reigning beauty but knows of her evil fame.
She is married—had sons and daughters when she humoured a
　Prince's whim;
But her husband is proud of her conquest—the Prince is a friend
　to *him*.

The bishop who christens her babies, the coachman who drives her
　pair,
The maid who carries her letters, the footman behind her chair,
The Marquis, her white-haired father, her brothers, so gossips say—
All know of the guilty passion of the Prince and the Countess May.

TWO WOMEN

The doors of the Court are open, and the great Lord Chamberlain bows,
Though he knows that the titled wanton has broken her marriage
vows;
And all of the courtiers flatter, and strive for a friendly glance—
On her whom the prince delights in who dares to look askance?

She is crowned with the world's fresh roses; no tongue has a word
of blame;
But the woman who falls from hunger is a thing too foul to name.
She is blessed who barters her honour just for a prince's smile;
The vice of the Court is *charming*, and the vice of the alley *vile*.

So, world, shall it be for ever—this hunting the street girl down,
While you honour the titled Phryne, and hold her in high renown;
But when, at the great uprising, they meet for the Judgment Day,
I'd rather be that drowned harlot than the beautiful Countess May.

THE ROAD TO HEAVEN

How is the boy this morning? Why do you shake your head?
Ah! I can see what's happened—there's a screen drawn round the bed.
So poor little Mike is sleeping the last long sleep of all;
I'm sorry—but who could wonder, after that dreadful fall?

Let me look at him, doctor—poor little London waif!
His frail barque's out of the tempest, and lies in God's harbour safe;
It's better he died in the ward here, better a thousand times,
Than have wandered back to the alley, with its squalor and nameless crimes.

THE ROAD TO HEAVEN

Too young for the slum to sully, he's gone to the wonderland
To look on the thousand marvels that he scarce could understand.
Poor little baby outcast, poor little waif of sin!
He has gone, and the pitying angels have carried the cripple in.

Didn't you know his story?—Ah, you weren't here, I believe,
When they brought the poor little fellow to the hospital, Christmas
    Eve.
It was I who came here with him, it was I who saw him go
Over the bridge that evening into the Thames below.

'Twas a raw cold air that evening—a biting Christmassy frost—
I was looking about for a collie—a favourite dog I'd lost.
Some ragged boys, so they told me, had been seen with one that night
In one of the bridge recesses, so I hunted left and right.

You know the stone recesses—with the long broad bench of stone,
To many a weary outcast as welcome as monarch's throne;
On the fiercest night you may see them, as crouched in the dark they
    lie,
Like the hunted vermin, striving to hide from the hounds in cry.

The seats that night were empty, for the morrow was Christmas Day,
And even the outcast loafers seemed to have slunk away;
They had found a warmer shelter—some casual ward, maybe—
They'd manage a morning's labour for the sake of the meat and tea.

I fancied the seats were empty, but, as I passed along,
Out of the darkness floated the words of a Christmas song,
Sung in a childish treble—'twas a boy's voice hoarse with cold,
Quavering out the anthem of angels and harps of gold.

I stood where the shadows hid me, and peered about until
I could see two ragged urchins, blue with the icy chill,
Cuddling close together, crouched on a big stone seat—
Two little homeless arabs, waifs of the London street.

One was singing the carol, when the other, with big round eyes—
It was Mike—looked up in wonder, and said, 'Jack, when we dies
Is that the place as we goes to—that place where ye'r dressed in white?
And has golding 'arps to play on, and it's warm and jolly and bright?

'Is that what they mean by 'eaven, as the misshun coves talks about,
Where the children's always happy and nobody kicks 'em out?'
Jack nodded his head assenting, and then I listened and heard
The talk of the little arabs—listened to every word.

Jack was a Sunday scholar, so I gathered from what he said,
But he sang in the road for a living—his father and mother were dead;
And he had a drunken granny, who turned him into the street—
She drank what he earned, and often he hadn't a crust to eat.

He told little Mike of heaven in his rough untutored way,
He made it a land of glory where the children sing all day;
And Mike, he shivered and listened, and told *his* tale to his friend,
How he was starved and beaten—'twas a tale one's heart to rend.

He'd a drunken father and mother, who sent him out to beg,
Though he'd just got over a fever, and was lame with a withered leg;
He told how he daren't crawl homeward, because he had begged in
     vain,
And his parents' brutal fury haunted his baby brain.

'I wish I could go to 'eaven,' he cried, as he shook with fright;
'If I thought as they'd only take me, why I'd go this very night.
Which is the way to 'eaven? How d'ye get there, Jack?'—
Jack climbed on the bridge's coping, and looked at the water black.

'That there's *one* road to 'eaven,' he said, as he pointed down
To where the cold Thames water surged muddy and thick and brown.
'If we was to fall in there, Mike, we'd be dead; and right through
    there
Is the place where it's always sunshine, and the angels has crowns
    to wear.'

Mike rose and looked at the water; he peered in the big broad stream,
Perhaps with a childish notion he might catch the golden gleam
Of the far-off land of glory. He leaned right over and cried—
'If them are the gates of 'eaven, how I'd like to be inside!'

He'd stood but a moment looking—how it happened I cannot tell—
When he seemed to lose his balance, gave a short shrill cry, and fell—
Fell o'er the narrow coping, and I heard his poor head strike
With a thud on the stonework under; then splash in the Thames went
   Mike.

       *   *   *   *

We brought him here that evening. For help I had managed to shout—
A boat put off from the landing, and they dragged his body out;
His forehead was cut and bleeding, but a vestige of life we found;
When they brought him here he was senseless, but slowly the child
   came round.

I came here on Christmas morning—the ward was all bright and gay
With mistletoe, green, and holly, in honour of Christmas Day;
And the patients had clean white garments, and a few in the room
   out there
Had joined in a Christmas service—they were singing a Christmas air.

They were singing a Christmas carol when Mike from his stupor woke,
And dim on his wandering senses the strange surroundings broke.
Half dreamily he remembered the tale he had heard from Jack—
The song, and the white-robed angels, the warm bright Heaven came
    back.

'I'm in Heaven,' he whispered faintly. 'Yes, Jack must have told me
    true!'
And, as he looked about him, came the kind old surgeon through.
Mike gazed at his face a moment, put his hand to his fevered head,
Then to the kind old doctor, 'Please, are you God?' he said.

Poor little Mike! 'twas Heaven, this hospital ward, to him—
A heaven of warmth and comfort, till the flickering lamp grew dim;
And he lay like a tired baby in a dreamless gentle rest,
And now he is safe for ever where such as he are best.

This is the day of scoffers, but who shall say that night,
When Mike asked the road to Heaven, that Jack didn't tell him right?
'Twas the children's Jesus pointed the way to the kingdom come
For the poor little tired arab, the waif of a London slum.

THE MATRON'S STORY

SHE was drunk—mad drunk—was Molly, the night that I saw
    her first;
    I'd seen some terrible cases, but hers was the very worst.
    This refuge had just been started for the daughters of night
and sin,
And I was the matron here, sir, on the night that they brought her in.

Her face was flushed and swollen, and a blow had cut her eye,
And the blood that had oozed unnoticed on her cheek was caked and
    dry.
She laughed with a hoarse, wild laughter, and capered and kicked
    about,
And she swore and she cursed so foully we thought we must turn
    her out.

She'd come for a spree, as often these poor lost creatures come.
They hear of our 'midnight meetings' away in their filthy slum;
I've seen 'em jump up on the platform and fling down the chairs and
    shriek,
And join in a ribald chorus when the clergyman tried to speak.

But Molly was worse than any — she staggered across the place
And picked up a brass-bound hymn-book and aimed at our chaplain's
    face;
It cut him across the cheek-bone, and he uttered a cry of pain,
Then we rushed at Molly to seize her, but she struggled with might
    and main.

She bit and she tore and scratched us, and kicked like a beast at bay,
Then all of a sudden reeled forward, and still as a mouse she lay;
In the struggle her wound was injured, and the blood flowed down
    apace,
And the same sort of mark we noticed was on hers and the chaplain's
    face.

What a fist had done for Molly the hymn-book had done for him;
He was only a young beginner, and he trembled in every limb;
For the wound was deep and painful, but he pushed his way through
    the crowd,
And cleared his voice with an effort, and spoke these words aloud:

'Poor lass may the Lord forgive her as I forgive her too!'
And silent, as if by magic, stood the whole of the yelling crew;
While he, with his face all bleeding, did the words of the Saviour
    quote,
That the left cheek should be offered to one who the right cheek
    smote.

THE MATRON'S STORY

He came where we held the wanton, and he moved his lips in prayer,
And smoothed from her bloody features the masses of tangled hair.
'Take her away,' he whispered, 'and see that her wound is drest,'
Then he spake aloud the blessing, and then he dismissed the rest.

We kept the girl at the Refuge right from the hour she swooned
Till time and a kindly surgeon had thoroughly healed the wound;
In a week it was closed completely, but leaving a mark to mar,
And the face of the poor lost creature and *his* had the self-same scar.

The day she was well she left us—left us with never a word;
Went back to the awful outcasts with whom such women herd;
And now and again we gathered news of the life she led:
'In the hospital,' once they told us, and then that the girl was dead.

It was five years after that, sir, one night went our faithful priest
On a mission of love and mercy to an awful place down East—
To a den where the lowest women herd with the vilest thieves—
They're some of the very worst, sir, that our Refuge here receives.

He'd heard from a girl who came here tales of this Devil's place,
And he made up his mind to storm it, armed with the word of Grace.
His face flushed red as he told us, and spoke of the souls to win.
And the task that the Lord had set him in that haven of shame and sin.

He laughed when we spoke of danger, and that night went forth
    alone,—
But we had a strange misgiving which we hardly liked to own;
He was back on the stroke of midnight—back from the jaws of hell,
But his face was pale and ghastly, he'd a strange wild tale to tell.

PREPARE TO SHED THEM NOW

He had entered that filthy alley and spoken God's Word aloud,
Till the people swarmed about him in a thick and threatening crowd;
And they jeered and they spat and hooted, and the women were worst
    of all,
For they picked up filth to pelt him, and drove him against the wall.

Beaten and bruised and smothered, he then would have turned and
    fled,
When a well-aimed brickbat struck him full on his hatless head.
Then he turned quite sick and giddy, and felt himself dragged along,
And a door was slammed in the faces of the threatening, murderous
    throng.

And beside him there stood a woman—he could hardly see her face,
For a foul and a noisome darkness hung o'er the dreadful place.
'Hush for your life!' she whispered, 'I've bolted and barred the door;
They'd 'ave your blood if I'd let 'em—hark, how the tigers roar!

'They found out as you're the parson as 'tices the gals away,
They say it's through you they peaches and goes on the "Christian"
    lay.
I dragged you in here and saved you, and sent out a gal for the slops*;
Ha, they're a-comin', sir! Listen! the noise and the shoutin' stops.'

The noise was changed in a moment to a hiss and a sullen groan,
The woman crept close and listened, then open the door was thrown,
And there was a sergeant standing with six of his tallest men,
And our chaplain walked between them out of that awful den.

---

*The police. The word—originally back slang, 'ecilop'—has passed into the ordinary
argot of the street.

And just as they reached the entry, lo, a woman's piercing shriek
Told of the brutal vengeance the ruffians tried to wreak.
He guessed what it was, did the sergeant, and hurrying back they
 found
The woman who'd saved our chaplain all of a heap on the ground.

The crowd in their brutal fury had beaten the woman down,
They kicked at her prostrate body till the red blood stained her gown;
But nobody knew who'd done it—the cowards had slunk away,
Her face was all white and ghastly in the light of the bull's-eye's ray.

'Twas the face of an old acquaintance our chaplain saw that night;
By the scar on the cheek he knew her, in the lantern's quivering light—
'Twas Molly, the long lost Molly, the girl that we thought was dead—
She beckoned him down and whispered, and these were the words
 she said :

'I know'd yer to-night by yer scar, sir, the scar o' the cut I made;
I heerd how yer treated me then, sir; how yer give me yer blessin'
 and prayed,
And I sez when I see yer in danger : Moll, you've a debt to pay,
So I dragged yer away in yonder, and I 'eld them curs at bay.'

Died ? No, she didn't; we saved her—she's matron here under me;
That's she—and ah, here comes the chaplain—now *both* the scars you
 can see.
And often we tell the story, how the Lord in His tender grace
Saved a life and a soul together all through a scar on the face.

KATE MALONEY

I N the winter, when the snowdrift stood against the cabin door,
Kate Maloney, wife of Patrick, lay nigh dying on the floor—
Lay on rags and tattered garments, moaning out with feeble
   breath,
'Knale beside me, Pat, my darlint; pray the Lord to give me death.'

Patrick knelt him down beside her, took her thin and wasted hand,
Saying something to her softly that she scarce could understand.
'Let me save ye, O my honey! Only spake a single word,
And I'll sell the goolden secret where it's wanted to be heard.

'Sure it cuts my heart to see ye lyin' dyin' day by day,
When it's food and warmth ye're wanting just to dhrive yer pains
   away.
There's a hundred goolden guineas at my mercy if ye will—
Do ye know that Mickey Regan's in the hut upon the hill?'

KATE MALONEY

Kate Maloney gripped her husband, then she looked him through
  and through;
'Pat Maloney, am I dhraming? Did I hear them words o' you?
Have I lived an honest woman, lovin' Ireland, God, and thee,
That now upon my deathbed ye should spake them words to me?

'Come ye here, ye tremblin' traitor; stand beside me now, and swear
By yer soul and yer hereafther, while he lives ye will not dare
Whisper e'en a single letter o' brave Mickey Regan's name.
Can't I die o' cold and hunger? Would ye have me die o' shame?

Let the Saxon bloodhounds hunt him, let them show their filthy gold;
What's the poor boy done to hurt 'em? Killed a rascal rich and old—
Shot an English thief who robbed us, grinding Irish peasants down,
Raisin' rints to pay his wantons and his lackeys up in town.

'We are beasts, we Irish peasants, whom these Saxon tyrants spurn;
If ye hunt a beast too closely, and ye wound him, won't he turn?
Wasn't Regan's sister ruined by the blackguard lying dead,
Who was paid his rint last Monday, not in silver, but in lead?'

Pat Maloney stood and listened, then he knelt and kissed his wife;
'Kiss me, darlint, and forgive me, sure I thought to save yer life;
And it's hard to see ye dyin' when the gold's within my reach.
I'll be lonely when ye're gone, dear,'—here a whimper stopped his
  speech.

       *   *   *   *

PREPARE TO SHED THEM NOW

Late that night, when Kate was dozing, Pat crept cautiously away
From his cabin to the hovel where the hunted Regan lay;
He was there—he heard him breathing; something whispered to him,
   'Go!
Go and claim the hundred guineas—Kate will never need to know.'

He would plan some little story when he brought her food to eat;
He would say the priest had met him, and had sent her wine and meat.
No one passed their lonely cabin; Kate would lie and fancy still
Mick had slipped away in secret from the hut upon the hill.

Kate Maloney woke and missed him; guessed his errand there and
   then;
Raised her feeble voice and cursed him with the curse of God and men.
From her rags she slowly staggered, took her husband's loaded gun,
Crying, 'God, I pray Thee, help me, ere the traitor's deed be done!'

All her limbs were weak with fever, as she crawled across the floor;
But she writhed and struggled bravely till she reached the cabin door,
Thence she scanned the open country, for the moon was in its prime,
And she saw her husband running, and she thought, 'There yet is
   time.

He had come from Regan's hiding, past the door, and now he went
By the pathway down the mountain, on his evil errand bent.
Once she called him, but he stopped not, neither gave he glance
   behind,
For her voice was weak and feeble, and it melted on the wind.

Then a sudden strength came to her, and she rose and followed fast,
Though her naked limbs were frozen by the bitter winter blast;
She had reached him very nearly when her newborn spirit fled.
'God has willed it!' cried the woman, *then she shot the traitor dead.*

From her bloodless lips, half frozen, rose a whisper to the sky,
 'I have saved his soul from treason; here, O Heaven, let me die.
Now no babe unborn shall curse him, nor his country loathe his name;
I have saved ye, O my husband, from a deed of deathless shame.'

No one yet has guessed their story; Mickey Regan got away,
And across the kind Atlantic lives an honest man to-day;
While in Galway still the peasants show the lonely mountain side
Where an Irishman was murdered and an Irishwoman died.

IN THE SIGNAL BOX

A STATIONMASTER'S STORY

YES, it's a quiet station, but it suits me well enough;
I want a bit of the smooth now, for I've had my share o'
  rough.
This berth that the company gave me, they gave as the
  work was light;
I was never fit for the signals after one awful night.
I'd been in the box from a younker, and I'd never felt the strain
Of the lives at my right hand's mercy in every passing train.
One day there was something happened, and it made my nerves go
  queer,
And it's all through that as you find me the station-master here.

136

IN THE SIGNAL BOX

I was on at the box down yonder—that's where we turn the mails,
And specials, and fast expresses, on to the centre rails;
The side's for the other traffic—the luggage and local slows.
It was rare hard work at Christmas, when double the traffic grows.
I've been in the box down yonder nigh sixteen hours a day,
Till my eyes grew dim and heavy, and my thoughts went all astray;
But I've worked the points half-sleeping—and once I slept outright,
Till the roar of the Limited woke me, and I nearly died with fright.

Then I thought of the lives in peril, and what might have been their
    fate
Had I sprung to the points that evening a tenth of a tick too late;
And a cold and ghastly shiver ran icily through my frame
As I fancied the public clamour, the trial, and bitter shame.
I could see the bloody wreckage—I could see the mangled slain—
And the picture was seared for ever, blood-red, on my heated brain.
That moment my nerve was shattered, for I couldn't shut out the
    thought
Of the lives I held in my keeping, and the ruin that might be wrought.

That night in our little cottage, as I kissed our sleeping child,
My wife looked up from her sewing, and told me, as she smiled,
That Johnny had made his mind up—he'd be a pointsman too.
'He says when he's big, like daddy, he'll work in the box with you.
I frowned, for my heart was heavy, and my wife she saw the look;
Lord bless you! my little Alice could read me like a book.
I'd to tell her of what had happened, and I said that I must leave,
For a pointsman's arm ain't trusty when terror lurks in his sleeve.

But she cheered me up in a minute, and that night, ere we went to
   sleep,
She made me give her a promise, which I swore that I'd always keep—
It was always to do my duty. 'Do that, and then, come what will,
You'll have no worry,' said Alice, 'if things go well or ill.
There's something that always tells us the thing that we ought to
   do'—
My wife was a bit religious, and in with the chapel crew.
But I knew she was talking reason, and I said to myself, says I,
'I won't give in like a coward—it's a scare that'll soon go by.'

Now, the very next day the missus had to go to the market town;
She'd the Christmas things to see to, and she wanted to buy a gown.
She'd be gone for a spell, for the parly didn't come back till eight,
And I knew, on a Christmas Eve, too, the trains would be extra late.
So she settled to leave me Johnny, and then she could turn the key—
For she'd have some parcels to carry, and the boy would be safe with
   me.
He was five was our little Johnny, and quiet, and nice, and good—
He was mad to go with daddy, and I'd often promised he should.

It was noon when the missus started—her train went by my box;
She could see, as she passed my window, her darling's curly locks.
I lifted him up to mammy, and he kissed his little hand,
Then sat, like a mouse, in the corner, and thought it was fairyland.
But somehow I fell a-thinking of a scene that would not fade,
Of how I had slept on duty, until I grew afraid;
For the thought would weigh upon me, one day I might come to lie
In a felon's cell for the slaughter of those I had doomed to die.

IN THE SIGNAL BOX

The fit that had come upon me, like a hideous nightmare seemed,
Till I rubbed my eyes and started like a sleeper who has dreamed.
For a time the box had vanished—I'd worked like a mere machine—
My mind had been on the wander, and I'd neither heard nor seen.
With a start I thought of Johnny, and I turned the boy to seek,
Then I uttered a groan of anguish, for my lips refused to speak;
There had flashed such a scene of horror swift on my startled sight
That it curdled my blood in terror and sent my red lips white.

It was all in one awful moment—I saw that the boy was lost:
He had gone for a toy, I fancied, some child from a train had tossed;
The local was easing slowly to stop at the station here,
And the Limited Mail was coming, and I had the line to clear.
I could hear the roar of the engine, I could almost feel its breath,
And right on the centre metals stood my boy in the jaws of death;
On came the fierce fiend, tearing straight for the centre line,
And the hand that must wreck or save it, O merciful God, was mine!

'Twas a hundred lives or Johnny's. O Heaven! what could I do?—
Up to God's ear that moment a wild, fierce question flew—
'What shall I do, O Heaven?' and sudden and loud and clear
On the wind came the words, 'Your duty,' borne to my listening ear.
Then I set my teeth, and my breathing was fierce and short and quick.
'My boy!' I cried, but he heard not; and then I went blind and sick;
The hot black smoke of the engine came with a rush before,
I turned the mail to the centre, and by it flew with a roar.

Then I sank on my knees in horror, and hid my ashen face—
I had given my child to Heaven; his life was a hundred's grace.
Had I held my hand a moment, I had hurled the flying mail
To shatter the creeping local that stood on the other rail!
Where is my boy, my darling? O God! let me hide my eyes.
How can I look—his father—on that which there mangled lies?
That voice!—O merciful Heaven!—'tis the child's, and he calls my
   name!
I hear, but I cannot see him, for my eyes are filled with flame.

I knew no more that night, sir, for I fell, as I heard the boy;
The place reeled round, and I fainted—swooned with the sudden joy.
But I heard on the Christmas morning, when I woke in my own warm
   bed,
With Alice's arms around me, and a strange wild dream in my head,
That she'd come by the early local, being anxious about the lad,
And had seen him there on the metals, and the sight nigh drove her
   mad—
She had seen him just as the engine of the Limited closed my view,
And she'd leapt on the line and saved him just as the mail dashed
   through.

She was back in the train in a second, and both were safe and sound—
The moment they stopped at the station she ran here, and I was found
With my eyes like a madman's glaring, and my face a ghastly white:
I heard the boy, and I fainted, and I hadn't my wits that night.
Who told me to do my duty? What voice was that on the wind?
Was it fancy that brought it to me? or were there God's lips behind?
If I hadn't a-done my duty—had I ventured to disobey—
My bonny boy and his mother might have died by my hand that day.

THE MAGIC WAND

A SCHOOL BOARD OFFICER'S STORY

HORRIBLE dens, sir, aren't they?
    This is one of my daily rounds
    It's here, in these awful places,
      That child-life most abounds.
We ferret from roof to basement
  In search of our tiny prey;
We're down on their homes directly
  If they happen to stop away.

PREPARE TO SHED THEM NOW

Knock at the door! Pooh, nonsense!
    They wouldn't know what it meant.
Come in and look about you;
    They'll think you're a School Board gent.
Did you ever see such hovels?
    Dirty, and damp, and small.
Look at the rotten flooring,
    Look at the filthy wall.

That's lucky—the place is empty,
    The whole of the family's out.
This is one of my fav'rite cases:
    Just give a glance about.
There's a father and four young children,
    And Sally the eldest's eight;
They're horribly poor—half-starving—
    And they live in a shocking state.

The father gets drunk and beats them,
    The mother she died last year:
There's a story about her dying
    I fancy you'd like to hear.
She was one of our backward pupils,
    Was Sally the eldest child—
A poor little London blossom
    The alley had not defiled.

142

THE MAGIC WAND

She was on at the Lane last winter—
   She played in the pantomime;
A lot of our School Board children
   Get on at the Christmas time.
She was one of a group of fairies,
   And her wand was the wand up there—
There, in the filthy corner
   Behind the broken chair.

The gilt of the star has faded,
   And the tinsel's peeled away;
But once, in the glaring lime-light,
   It gleamed like a jewelled spray.
A fairy's wand in a lodging
   In a slum like this looks queer;
But you'll guess why they let her keep it
   When you know how the wand came here.

Her mother was ill that winter,
   Her father, the drunken sot,
Was spending his weekly earnings
   And all that the fairy got.
The woman lay sick and moaning,
   Dying by slow degrees
Of a cruel and wasting fever
   That rages in dens like these.

143

PREPARE TO SHED THEM NOW

But night after night went Sally,
   Half starved, to the splendid scene
Where she waved a wand of magic
   As a Liliput fairy queen.
She stood in the 'Land of Shadows'
   Where a demon worked his spell,
At a wave of her wand he vanished,
   And the scene was changed as well.

She'd a couple of lines to utter,
   Which bade the gloom give way
To the 'Golden Home of Blisses
   In the Land of the Shining Day.
She gazed on the limelit splendours
   That grew as she waved her wand,
And she thought of the cheerless cellar
   Old Drury's walls beyond.

And when, in her ragged garments,
   No longer a potent fay,
She knelt by the wretched pallet
   Where her dying mother lay.
She thought, as she stooped and kissed her,
   And looked in the ghastly face,
Of the wand that could change a dungeon
   To a sweet and lovely place.

THE MAGIC WAND

She was only a wretched outcast,
  A waif of the London slums;
It's little of truth and knowledge
  To the ears of such children comes.
She fancied her wand was truly
  Possessed of a magic charm,
That it punished the wicked people,
  And shielded the good from harm.

Her mother grew slowly weaker,
  The depth of the winter came,
And the teeth of the biting weather
  Seized on the wasted frame.
And Sally, who saw her sinking,
  Came hom from the Lane one night
With her shawl wrapped over something,
  And her face a ghostly white.

She had hidden the wand and brought it,
  The wand that could do so much;
She crept to the sleeping woman,
  Who moved not at her touch.
She stooped to hear her breathing,
  It was, O, so fair and low;
Then, raising her wand, she waved it,
  Like a fairy, to and fro.

145

PREPARE TO SHED THEM NOW

Her well-known lines she uttered,
　　That bade the gloom give way
To 'The Golden Home of Blisses
　　In the Land of Shining Day.'
She murmured, 'O mother, dearest,
　　You shall look on the splendid scene!'
While a man from the playhouse watched her
　　Who'd followed the fairy queen.

He thought she had stolen something,
　　And brought it away to sell,
He had followed her home and caught her
　　And then he'd a tale to tell.
He told how he watched her waving
　　The wand by her mother's bed,
O'er a face where the faint grey shadows
　　Of the last long sleep had spread.

She's still at the school, is Sally,
　　And she's heard of the Realms of Light;
So she clings to the childish fancy
　　That entered her head that night.
She says that her poor sick mother
　　By her wand was charmed away
From earth to the Home of Blisses
　　In the Land of Eternal Day.

THE LEVEL CROSSING

THE eight o'clock up's just gone, sir—the London express, you mean?
  There ain't not another as stops here, not till the nine-fifteen.
  Got any luggage a-comin'?—Oh, only been here for the day.
Yes, it's a quietish village; never was over-gay.
We're glad of a stranger sometimes, and a bit of the Lunnon news;
It's lonely up here at the station, and easy to get the blues,
For I'm on till the early morning; and many and many a night
There's never a human being as comes to bless my sight.

For the last of the trains as stops here is the parly at 10 pm,
And then I'm alone with my thoughts like, and I ain't always fond
    o' them.
Out yonder's a level crossing, and it's part o' my work, you know,
To watch here at night for the waggons a-travellin' to and fro.
Been any accidents? Bless you! we're a boon to the local Press;
The Company has me stop here just to try for to make 'em less.
Why, only last year a farmer—but haven't you heard the tale
How old Farmer Burton o' Birley was killed by the Limited Mail?

I thought as you must ha' heard it, for it made a regular fuss,
And they held an inquiry on it, and they laid the blame on us.
We ought to ha' seen and ha' warned him, so the chaps on the paper
    said;
But we none of us knew as he'd got there, not till we see him dead.
They brought it in accidental, the jury as tried the case;
But it was no accident neither, though it's rather a likely place.
Come and sit down in my shanty, you've nearly an hour to wait,
If you care for the rest I can tell you the story of Burton's fate.

Never mind how I know it—there's plenty o' folks beside
As knows about Master Burton, and why he came here and died;
For the women ha' talked it over, and whenever that comes about,
Wherever there's secrets hidden, the women ''ll hunt 'em out.
They wagged their heads when he married poor penniless Mercy Leigh
Right on the top of her hearin' as her lover was drowned at sea.
Lord, how the women chattered—scandalous things they said!
Hintin' she wanted a husband to hide her sin with the dead!

THE LEVEL CROSSING

This Mercy Leigh was the daughter of decentish honest folks,
And Burton had made her an offer, but she treated his words as jokes,
For Mercy was barely twenty, and Burton was sixty-two;
He'd made a bit at the farmin', and was counted as well to do;
He made it a joke himself like, his love for 'the pretty child,'
And if anyone chaffed him about it, that's what he said, and smiled;
But under his broad thick waistcoat, right in his kind old heart,
I know as her nonsense pained him, though he took it in right good
    part.

It was pretty well known in the village that Mercy had set her cap
At the son of old Barnes, the builder, a dare-devil sailor chap;
And when he was off his cruises, and home for a week or so,
You'd meet him and Mercy together wherever you'd chance to go.
And the last time they parted he told her—that's what the gossips
    say—
That he reckoned, with luck and weather, he'd be but a month
    away,
And when he came back he'd wed her—he pledged her his solemn
    word;—
He'd perished at sea with his vessel—that was the next we heard.

Now, the very next day this Mercy was seen, with a long white face,
A-makin' for Chumleigh Meadows—that was old Burton's place—
And one of his people told me as she stayed there half the day,
And they heard her a-cryin' and sobbin', and moanin' her heart away.
But when they came out the farmer had gotten her hand gripped tight,
And he kissed her, and said, 'God bless you! I'll speak to your folks
    to-night.'
It was known on the morrow through Birley that Mercy had promised
    to wed
The farmer of Chumleigh Meadows—but we noticed her eyes were
    red.

'Twas plain as her heart was buried away in the distant sea,

For I saw her the weddin' mornin', and her looks had a tale for me.

But she went through the service bravely, and the farmer's big brown face

Was bright with his love for Mercy, though he stood in a dead man's place.

I think they was happy at first, too, for he worshipped the ground she trod,

And went here and there like a sheep-dog, obeyin' her every nod.

Yet he'd given his name and honour to a woman who'd told him—well,

What seldom to one who'd wed her a woman has dared to tell.

THE LEVEL CROSSING

They were married six months and over, when, all of a sudden, flew
News through the streets of Birley, as nobody thought was true,—
That Barnes had escaped the shipwreck, and was back from a length-
ened trip;
He'd been rescued and carried to Melbourne aboard of a sailin' ship.
She heard it first at the station—I shall never forget her cry.
We carried her into this room here—I thought she was like to die;
But she got all right in a minit, and, takin' her husband's arm,
She walked like a tipsy woman back thro' the fields to the farm.

In less than a month from that, sir, old Burton lay here dead;
Here, at this level crossing—'Accident,' so they said.
But I know, for the woman told me who'd seen her before the 'quest,
That for many a night he'd murmur, and talk in his troubled rest;
And he'd wake in the night, and tell her, if it chanced that he should
die,
That the hand of God would have freed her for a higher and holier tie.
And the eve as it happened he kissed her, with tears in his eyes, and
said,
'Mercy, my darling! remember the *reason* that we were wed.'

When he left her that night he told her he'd a lawyer to see in town.
He was crossing there for the platform when the engine struck him
down.
That's how the jury got it, but *I* know a thing or two;
And I say that night when he kissed her, he knew what he meant to do;
For his will was made, and it told her to marry the sailor chap
If it pleased the Almighty to take him—accident too, mayhap?
She went away from the village, and the farm and the house were sold,
And she'd married young Barnes ere her mourning was barely a
fortnight old.

A cold-blooded thing to do, sir?—Not a bit of it. She was right;
For she knew what was wearing his heart out when he went to his
    death that night.
He laid down his life that a father, cast up from the jaws of the sea,
Might hallow before God's altar the mother of one to be.
It was just a month to the day, sir, since Burton was found here dead,
That the baby was born to Mercy.—Why, bless us! the lights are red!
I must run to the box and change 'em. What does that signal mean?
Why, that I must be saying good-night, sir, for here is the nine-fifteen.

Grey haired, sparse of hair, or actually bald, you stand at a tremendous disadvantage in life. Nothing detracts from youthful appearance so much as lack of hair. Yet there is no form of offended nature so easy of cure.

Mr. George R. Sims

made it so. He himself was exercised when he found a tendency to baldness. But not for long. With the assistance of medical specialists of his acquaintance he discovered a cure. That cure he registered under the title of 'Tatcho.' 'Tatcho' solved his difficulty. 'Tatcho' will solve yours. There is a reason why 'Tatcho' should appeal to everybody—to business men and women a very special reason. That reason is the appalling effect greyness, loss of hair, or actual baldness exercises on

Business Life.

This has occupied the serious attention of the Press and trade organs of nearly every industry in the kingdom. Those who have studied the trend of customs enforced in our largest commercial houses will tell you that to a greater extent than even mental and physical incapacity, greyness and baldness have been

The Knockout Blow

to thousands of careers. Now those engaged in pursuits in which youthful appearance is a *sine qua non* (and in what business is it not ?) cannot do better than take the cue from His Majesty's Army and Navy. Officers high in authority say that greyness and baldness are, thanks to 'Tatcho' now practically unknown both in officers and rank and file.

" *You remember,*" says Mr. Geo. R. Sims in the *Referee,* to the Editor, " *that you yourself were using a preparation that did you no good. Then I made you up a bottle of* 'Tatcho.' *Look at the difference now, sir !*"

Write to-day for your 4/6 Trial Bottle of 'TATCHO,' 1/10 Carr. Paid.